QAR Now

QUESTION
ANSWER
RELATIONSHIPS

Taffy E. Raphael

Kathy Highfield

Kathryn H. Au

■SCHOLASTIC

NEW YORK • TORONTO • LONDON • AUCKLAND • SYDNEY
MEXICO CITY • NEW DELHI • HONG KONG • BUENOS AIRES

KH

Dedication

To teachers and students,
from whom we've learned so much.

Cover design by Maria Lilja
Interior design by Sarah Morrow
Photographs courtesy of the authors

"Qillak" and "Surfing the Sky" from Super QAR for Testwise Students © copyright 2001
by Taffy Raphael and Kathryn Au (2001). Published by the Wright Group, a division of McGraw-Hill
Excerpt from FCAT reprinted from the FCAT 2001 test released item bank.

11/21/06

2 3 4 5 6 7 8 9 10 40 12 11 10 09 08 07 06

Contents

Acknowledgments

We'd like to thank the following educators and students for the invaluable help they gave us as we wrote this book.

Tammy Nakagawa, Holomua Elementary School, Ewa, Hawaii

Kristin Terstriep, Revere Elementary School, Chicago, Illinois

Janine Rodrigues, Gray Elementary School, Chicago, Illinois

Jennifer McClorey, James Shields Elementary School, Chicago, Illinois

Hannah Natividad, James Shields Elementary School, Chicago, Illinois

Melissa Tischler, Pulaski School, Chicago, Illinois

Pam Coke, Colorado State University

Laura Pardo, Lansing, Michigan

Leah Werab, Oscar Mayer Elementary, Chicago, Illinois

Maria Ruiz Blanco, Belmont-Cragin School, Chicago Illinois

Chanmi Lim's fifth-grade class, Boone Elementary School, Chicago, Illinois

Karen Marfise, James Shields Elementary School, Chicago, Illinois

Sandra Traback, Principal, Cesar Chavez Elementary School, Chicago, Illinois

Pat Winger, Cesar Chavez Elementary School, Chicago, Illinois

Rosa Gonzalez, Cesar Chavez Elementary School, Chicago, Illinois

Partnership READ, University of Illinois at Chicago (funded through the Searle Funds of the Chicago Community Trust)

Rita Gardner, Principal (retired), James Shields Elementary School, Chicago, Illinois

Jean Nielsen, James Shields Elementary School, Chicago, Illinois

Milagros Vazzano, James Shields Elementary School, Chicago, Illinois

Marelyn Manliguis, Kipapa Elementary School, Mililani, Hawaii

Kim Nakamura, Kipapa Elementary School, Mililani, Hawaii

Manford Realin, Kipapa Elementary School, Mililani, Hawaii

Laura Sakai, Kipapa Elementary School, Mililani, Hawaii

Karen Mangin, James Shields Elementary School, Chicago, Illinois

Victor Arroyo, James Shields Elementary School, Chicago, Illinois

Foreword

by P. David Pearson

It is always a privilege—and quite easy—to recommend a useful book. On those grounds alone, I was pleased to be asked to write a foreword for such a profoundly useful book. Teachers, administrators, and teacher educators will find lots of good ideas for making QARs happen in their classrooms, schools, and internship programs.

It is doubly a privilege when the book is not only useful but also based on solid theory and research. Born of the revolution in our understanding of reading in the late 1970s, Question Answer Relationships (QARs, or *kwars* as some kids call them) are a direct outcome of the time Taffy and I, along with Kathy Au and a host of others, spent immersed in the new ideas of schema theory (Anderson, Spiro, & Montague, 1977) and script theory (Schank & Abelson, 1977), thinking about how they related to comprehension instruction (Durkin, 1978; Pearson & Johnson, 1978). As Taffy and her colleagues discuss in the introduction, it was in this milieu that Taffy had the idea of finding a way to make explicit to kids a process that usually only scholars described. This was a breakthrough for Taffy, and it led ultimately to a breakthrough for thousands of teachers around the country. What teachers liked about QAR was the language—having words that enabled them to label, discuss, dissect, and analyze these slippery ideas with their students. But the point is that both the theory (the fundamental idea that reading involves a reader making connections between his or her own knowledge, the ideas in a text, and the author who wrote the text) and the research documenting the efficacy of QARs have widened, deepened, and withstood the test of time.

The privilege is compounded even more when one has a close professional and personal relationship with the authors. I had the good fortune of meeting the three authors when each was a doctoral student in reading and language. I have followed the work that the three of them have done separately and in pairs, and I admire it all. The work that Kathy Au did with the Kamehameha Early Education Project (KEEP) still serves as a model of what culturally responsive (and responsible) pedagogy is all about. Taffy's work on Book Club, of course, is seminal. Kathy Highfield joined Taffy in an offshoot of Book Club, called Book Club Plus, with the explicit goal of bringing the key elements of Book Club into an age of standards and consequential assessments. And Kathy Au and Taffy have each been involved in implementing a version of standards-based reform (Taffy in Chicago and Kathy in Hawaii) that brings together many of these common threads. What is special about *QAR Now* is that here these threads from the authors' individual and collective earlier work are woven into the QAR curriculum they have built for us as readers and teachers. (In fact, it might be more accurate to say that QAR is woven into the earlier work.) So we read about how QARs can be adapted to standards, correlated with state outcomes, or used to prepare kids to take state tests. We see that they can be embedded easily into a Book Club curriculum by sharpening students' ability to ask different sorts of questions at different points in the reading of a chapter book. We also see that QAR instruction can be enhanced when it is conceptualized within a sociocultural view of learning (the Vygotsky Space in Chapter 2). As I said, I am not sure that QAR is woven into these earlier threads or vice-versa. But in either case, the weaving works to produce a sturdy and attractive "whole cloth."

Finally, the privilege is raised to an even higher level (I think we're at the 4th power!) when the topic is so important, the information so relevant, and the stakes for ignoring the message so high. We live and work during a curricular age in which, once again, we are reaching back to the "basics" to make sure that kids know their ABCs (now augmented by phonemic awareness), have acquired their phonics skills, and can read fluently. That is all well and good (I have nothing against knowing the code or reading fluently), but those basics won't take us far enough. They won't get individual students or our nation to the "proficient" level on NAEP that these authors discuss in their introduction. To meet that challenge, to prepare for the life of reason, critical analysis, and good citizenship that we hold as aspirations for all of our children, we'll have to stretch a little, maybe a lot, further. Instead of thinking about comprehension as a magic box where "a miracle occurs," we'll have to think about it as a complex process that can be unpacked, unmasked, and brought out for public inspection— so that all students, and especially those who really do think it is a miracle, can see how it works. That's the key to this book—its authors are helping teachers, and ultimately their students, learn how to unpack the black box of comprehension so that they can all see, up close and personal, how it works. What's even better is that when the three of them take us on this journey to the center of the mind, they are wonderful tour guides.

So enjoy the adventure! And when you finish, you too will be qualified to lead that very same journey. And may your students enjoy the intellectual adventure for which you will serve as their tour guide.

Introduction

In the late 1970s, disquieting information about classroom literacy instruction was being uncovered, while at the same time remarkable understandings about how we learn from text were being discovered. Dolores Durkin's now classic study had just appeared in *Reading Research Quarterly* (Durkin, 1978–79), documenting how rarely comprehension instruction occurred in the classroom. At the same time, concepts we take for granted today, including schema theory (Anderson & Pearson, 1984) and metacognition (Brown, Campione, & Day, 1981), were being introduced and applied to comprehension instruction in books such as *Teaching Reading Comprehension* by P. David Pearson and Dale Johnson (1978). Despite this growing body of research on comprehension, there was much to learn about comprehension-strategy instruction.

It was in this climate that Question Answer Relationships— QAR—was born from a research project involving second- through eighth-grade students. Taffy Raphael—the creator of QAR—was a graduate student working as a research assistant to David Pearson. Pearson was one of the scholars deeply involved in linking the theoretical work of the Center for the Study of Reading at the University of Illinois at Urbana-Champaign to the world of classroom instruction. Pearson served as a mentor and adviser to many graduate students at that time, guiding them to focus on different aspects of comprehension instruction, such as developing strategies, understanding comprehension assessment, and identifying effective teaching practices. Taffy had become particularly interested in the questioning practices that seemed to be the basis of so much of the research and strategy work. Almost everyone doing comprehension research used questions to evaluate what students had learned. We all took for granted that being able to answer questions was a clear and valid indication that students had understood the text.

But Taffy saw student responses to questions that concerned her. She noticed students who appeared to ignore completely the texts they had just read as they struggled to answer questions. They never looked back at the source that could have helped them answer a question easily. Others spent inordinate amounts of time rereading, when questions could have been answered easily from their prior experiences. Taffy was also concerned about the questions students were asked. Questions were usually categorized as literal or inferential, based on the words in the question alone—often with reference to Bloom's taxonomy. For example, a question that began with *why* was identified as inferential, even when the answer to the question was clearly stated in the text. Questions beginning with *what* were sometimes labeled as low-level factual questions when, in fact, answering them required students to integrate text extensively and to make inferences.

Perhaps not surprisingly—she was David's student—Taffy was drawn to a different system of categorizing questions that Pearson and Johnson (1978) had developed. They argued that the difficulty level of a question could be judged only in light of the task demands of the question and the source or sources of information the reader would need to use to answer it. They laid out three categories of questions:

Text Explicit	Text Implicit	Script Implicit
The information necessary to answer the question is located in a single place in the text. The reader would have to search for the information but would not have to engage in inferential thinking.	The information necessary to answer the question is in the text, but the reader would need to engage in inferential thinking or, at the minimum, make intertextual connections.	Answers come from the reader's schema—the "scripts" we have in our brains that help us recognize familiar situations and use what we know to answer a new question.

These three categories formed the basis for Taffy's original series of research studies (Raphael & McKinney, 1983; Raphael & Pearson, 1985; Raphael & Wonnacott, 1985), in which she explored the essential questions:

* In what ways does knowing about the relationship between the question, the text to which the question refers, and the readers' knowledge base help readers more effectively respond to comprehension questions after reading?

* How can we teach QAR effectively?

Because the language of the Pearson and Johnson taxonomy was so theoretical, Taffy renamed the categories Right There (Text Explicit), Think & Search (Text Implicit), and On My Own (Script Implicit) and called these categories Question Answer Relationships, or QAR. This categorization system has been refined and instructional applications of it have been extended to a range of purposes for more than two decades. In fact, the staying power of QAR has been quite remarkable. Teachers use it in a variety of ways across grade levels and in a range of subject areas. Its simplicity makes it is accessible to beginning teachers and beginning readers and yet useful to the most experienced teachers and their students of all levels.

Why publish this book now? Our work with QAR for the last 25 years has shown us that QAR can successfully address four important issues (Raphael & Au, 2005).

1. **Teachers and students have difficulty communicating effectively about problems with comprehension and questions.**

QAR addresses this challenge by giving teachers and students a shared language to make visible the largely invisible process underlying reading comprehension. More than anything else, it is this shared language that seems to account for the staying power of QAR. The original work with QAR centered on the use of the question categories in classrooms and the ways that QAR allowed teachers and students to address issues related to questions and reading comprehension. QAR illuminates the relationship between questioning and reading comprehension for both teachers and students. With innovative, student-centered literacy activities such as inquiry projects and book clubs—as well as higher standards for students' thinking—the emphasis in many classrooms has shifted from teacher-generated questions to student-generated questions. The shared language of QAR facilitates this shift.

2. Nearly all schools need to develop a coherent framework for comprehension instruction.

Many teachers recognize the importance of comprehension instruction but are uncertain about what the appropriate focus should be at their grade level and about how to get started. QAR can bring coherence to literacy instruction within and across grade levels because it provides a framework with a developmental progression for comprehension instruction. Teachers can use this framework to plan questioning activities and organize instruction in comprehension strategies that cut across subject areas. The shared language of QAR makes this framework possible.

3. Students need to be prepared for high-stakes tests.

In many districts teachers find themselves under pressure to raise test scores, and as a result, some have narrowed the curriculum to spend months at a time on test preparation. In our opinion, this narrowing has taken the joy out of teaching and causes students to receive an inferior education. The short-term goal of scoring high on tests has taken precedence over the long-term goal of gaining reading comprehension strategies of lasting value in school and in life. We think that QAR allows schools to have the best of both worlds: It prepares students for the tests while making sure that they have strategies for engaging in higher-level thinking and reasoning with text. These strategies can be applied in a wide range of situations, not only in school but also in the community and workplace.

4. **Schools need support as they begin sustained, whole-school change to improve their students' literacy achievement, particularly their higher-level thinking with text.**

While QAR started as a way to help individual teachers and their students, its developmental progression allows it to be used to pull a whole school together around reading comprehension instruction. Each grade level builds on the steps accomplished in the previous year and prepares students for the steps they must take the following year. Such a "staircase" curriculum can be particularly beneficial in schools with students of diverse backgrounds, where struggling learners typically receive little or no reading comprehension instruction or do not receive such instruction until the later grades.

We believe QAR can provide significant benefits to schools, teachers, and students for a relatively small investment of time and energy. For schools, QAR provides a way into comprehension instruction on a school-wide basis. For teachers, QAR serves as a means of framing, planning, and providing instruction in reading comprehension and questioning activities. For students, QAR leads to success with generating and answering questions, facilitates reasoning, and promotes learning across the content areas. Many educational innovations are complex and costly. In contrast, QAR provides a straightforward and powerful framework that provides significant, almost immediate benefits to schools, teachers, and, most important, our students, who must face the complex demands of the future.

Chapter 1

Understanding Question Answer Relationships

*W*hile reading aloud *Sarah Plain and Tall* by Patricia MacLachlan (HarperTrophy, 1987) to her third-grade students, Kathy Highfield asked questions such as: "What kinds of animals do you think Sarah's going to find when she gets to the farm?" "Do you think Sarah is going to stay? Why or why not?" "How would you feel if you were Sarah?" Many of Kathy's students shrugged when she asked these questions. Some responded by saying, "I don't know. Keep reading and we'll find out."

Despite the fact that students ask and answer questions from the time they are toddlers, in school settings they are often ineffective in applying comprehension strategies for answering them. For many of these students, this poor and passive performance during classroom discussions stems from a lack of understanding about sources of information for answering and asking questions. This problem is what Question Answer Relationships (QAR) was designed to address. QAR is a comprehension strategy that provides a way to think and talk about sources of information for answering questions. The language of QAR and the accessibility of the concepts underlying it provide teachers with a way to meet the rising expectations for higher levels of thinking in our increasingly diverse schools.

In this chapter, we set a context for why QAR is particularly relevant given current expectations for teachers and students to meet the highest standards for achievement. We introduce the QAR categories and provide examples of ways you can get off to a strong start with QAR instruction.

Greater Accountability, Rising Expectations

There are many reasons we want our students to meet the highest standards for literacy achievement. Our democratic society depends on an informed citizenry, one capable of thinking critically, evaluating information, understanding what is explicitly stated and what needs to be inferred, and thinking deeply about what other questions need to be asked. Capable citizens need to be able to interpret what they are reading and draw conclusions based on evidence. We want our students to be able to enjoy high levels of literacy both for personal satisfaction and to achieve success in an increasingly information-based economy. For educators there is also an important immediate reason. Teachers, schools, and districts today are faced with a harsh reality: If their students are unable to perform well on high-stakes state tests, the districts, schools, and teachers—not just the students—are labeled as failing.

Clearly, finding a way to improve students' abilities to understand questioning is more important than ever. However, as Taffy Raphael and Clydie Wonnacott (1985) found, simply practicing answering questions did not lead to improved student performance. Instead, as Barbara Taylor and her colleagues found, students must engage in high levels of questioning and do so in highly interactive settings to achieve high levels of comprehension (Taylor, Pearson, Peterson, & Rodriguez, 2003, 2005).

Likewise, teachers must know what is expected of their students in terms of comprehension.

Fortunately, much has been written lately that describes what it means to comprehend text successfully (e.g., Pressley, 2002; Sweet & Snow, 2003). The RAND report, for example, commissioned by the United States Department of Education, states that proficiency is achieved when a reader can

* read a variety of materials with ease and interest,

* read for varying purposes,

* read with comprehension even when the material is neither easy to understand nor intrinsically interesting,

* acquire new knowledge and understand new concepts,

* apply textual information appropriately,

* reflect on what is being read.

The National Assessment of Educational Progress (NAEP, 2003) is the only federally funded large-scale testing program in the United States. Many state tests align with the NAEP framework, and the framework for the NAEP 2009 reading assessment (NAEP, 2004) reveals a trend toward even higher expectations than the RAND report specified. Specifically, students will be expected to be comfortable reading a range of genres, such as fiction, nonfiction, procedural texts, and poetry. Seventy to eighty percent of the questions on the NAEP assessment will require that students integrate, interpret, critique, and evaluate texts read independently. Fewer than a third of the questions will simply require readers to locate and recall information.

Further, over half of the higher-level questions will require short or extended written responses, rather than being in a multiple-choice format. In the fiction category, students must write in response to questions about themes, analyze elements of various plot structures, and write from multiple perspectives. For nonfiction texts, students will need to use what they know about how information is organized (e.g., compare-contrast, problem-solution, explanation) to identify important details and themes using text, graphs, photos, and other features. This range of strategic knowledge is central to high levels of literacy achievement, whether in formal testing situations or in everyday contexts in and out of school.

Meeting the Needs of All Students

If trends continue, an ever increasing gap in literacy achievement between mainstream students and students of diverse backgrounds will remain a central concern in our work as educators (Au, 2003). We use the term *diverse* here to refer to ethnicity, socioeconomic status, and primary language. In the United States, for example, students of diverse backgrounds may be African American, Latino, or Native American in ethnicity; come from low-income families; or speak African American vernacular English or Spanish as their primary language (Au, 1993). The reading test results from the 2002 NAEP reveal a disturbing achievement gap between students of diverse backgrounds and mainstream students (Grigg, Daane, Jin, & Campbell, 2003). The results displayed in Table 1.1 show that by twelfth grade, as a group, students from diverse backgrounds have fallen four years behind their mainstream peers.

The average twelfth-grade black student's score (267) is the same as the average eighth-grade Asian/Pacific Islander student's (267) and slightly below that of the average eighth-grade white student's (272). An average twelfth-grade Hispanic student's score (273) is only one point above that of an average eighth-grade white student's. This gap begins in elementary school and continues to widen over time.

While there are many explanations for the literacy achievement gap within and beyond the purview of classroom teachers, our focus is on

Table 1.1 *Average 2002 NAEP Reading Scores*

Ethnicity	Grade 4	Grade 8	Grade 12
White	229	272	292
Black	199	245	267
Hispanic	201	247	273
Asian/Pacific Islander	224	267	286

what is within their control: the currently limited opportunities diverse students have for high-quality instruction in reading comprehension. Researchers such as Linda Darling-Hammond (1995) and Jill Fitzgerald (1995) have documented that, when compared to their mainstream peers, students of diverse backgrounds tend to receive a great deal of instruction in lower-level skills and little instruction in reading comprehension and higher-level thinking about text. One reason for this disparity—lowered expectations for the achievement of students of diverse backgrounds—is something we can change. Jeannie Oakes and Gretchen Guiton (1995) suggest that these lowered expectations reflect the mistaken belief that students of diverse backgrounds are less capable of higher-level thinking than mainstream students. These findings suggest that educators must be careful to guard against thinking that instruction in lower-level skills is somehow a better match for the abilities of students of diverse backgrounds. Another mistaken belief is that students must master the basics before being introduced to higher-level strategies. When struggling readers eventually master basic skills, they find they have missed perhaps years of opportunities to learn and use more complex strategies and they still lag behind their peers.

Research clearly shows that all students need instruction in reading comprehension, especially teaching that focuses on the strategies required to answer and generate challenging questions (Taylor et al., 2003, 2005). As we described above, in the near future a high proportion of test questions will require students to use higher-level thinking, such as making reader-text connections and examining the content and structure of the text (National Assessment Governing Board, 2004; National Center for Educational Statistics, 2003). If students of diverse backgrounds do not receive the kind of comprehension instruction that can prepare them for assessments increasingly oriented toward higher-level thinking with text, we have little hope of being able to close the achievement gap.

In our work in schools with a high proportion of students of diverse backgrounds, we have found that teachers may be unsure how to change long-standing patterns of instruction in lower-level skills. They may be unsure of how to teach different comprehension strategies in a way that allows students to see how the strategies work together to facilitate understanding. The consequences of lower levels of instruction extend far beyond low test scores, and students of diverse backgrounds are likely to be particularly hard hit. They will face limited opportunities for higher education, employment, and overall advancement in the larger society (Raphael & Au, 2005).

We believe that QAR can provide a practical and theoretically sound way to ensure that all our students have access to instruction in higher-level literacy and critical thinking. The concepts underlying QAR and the language for talking about these concepts are accessible to teachers and to students of diverse backgrounds, ages, and ability levels. We find that with this language, teachers and students have the means for organizing comprehension instruction and critical thinking strategies. The language of QAR provides continuity across subject areas and grade levels as well.

QAR: A Language for Comprehension Instruction

Let's examine QAR in more depth. Question Answer Relationships has been described as a comprehension strategy or a metacognitive strategy (see, for example, Raphael, 1986), but first and foremost it is a language for use in the classroom. It provides a common way of thinking about and talking about sources of information for answering questions.

Figure 1.1 *The Primary Question Answer Relationships*

In the Book   In My Head

QAR Now: Question Answer Relationships

Whether you work with kindergartners or adolescents, struggling readers or highly successful ones, the QAR language you use is the same. The language conveys the idea that answers can be found in text sources (from traditional texts to new technologies) or in our background knowledge and experiences—In the Book or In My Head QARs, respectively. (See Figure 1.1.) Over the years we've learned how important it is for students to understand the distinction between these two primary sources of information. Only then can they move into the more fine-grained analyses within each category.

Getting Started: Introducing Two Primary Information Sources

Tammy Nakagawa at Holomua Elementary School in Ewa, Hawaii, used QAR to help her special-education students. In particular, she wanted her students to understand what an information source was and how information from external sources can become part of one's background knowledge. She first used the QAR language of In My Head and In the Book to bring her students' attention to the wide array of information sources available to them on a daily basis in and out of school. To help her students, she created the chart shown in Figure 1.2.

Figure 1.2

Chart Identifying Sources of Information

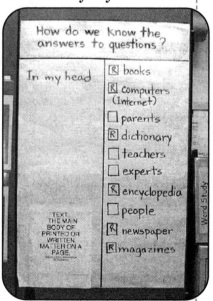

In the right-hand column of the chart she listed the many sources of information that students identified. After they had brainstormed this list, Tammy added the small box next to each source. In their next discussion, they identified which of the sources could be read. Those were marked with a red *R*. The chart helped her students reflect both on the range of sources and on how information in our head develops from external sources.

When Kristin Terstriep, from Revere Elementary School in Chicago, saw a photograph of Tammy's chart, she decided to use it with her third-grade students. Though the type of students she was working with and the environment they were in was very different from Tammy's, she found that grounding her students' introduction to QAR in a conversation about knowledge sources was a powerful way to begin. This conversation helped keep students' attention focused on what she considered to be a crucial aspect of learning—that what is new to us today becomes our background knowledge and experiences of the future. She also believes the conversation helped her students to understand that QAR is more than simply choosing the correct type of relationship. Rather, QAR can actually lead to an understanding of how knowledge develops. Kristin made sure her students had a solid understanding of the two primary sources of information before moving on to subsequent QAR categories. For example, she involved students in reflecting on what they had learned so they could display their understandings to others. To do this, she asked her students to convey their understanding of the primary sources of information by drawing a picture. Figure 1.3 displays two of Kristin's students' illustrations—In the Book and In My Head.

Like Tammy and Kristin, Janine Rodrigues teaches Question Answer Relationships to her students—first graders at Gray Elementary School in Chicago, Illinois. Janine first makes sure that her students are able to distinguish between the primary information sources. For

Figure 1.3 *Students' Visualizations of the Primary QARs*

example, she may ask them to demonstrate what they've learned by generating a question from each category after listening to a Read Aloud or by identifying the QAR they used to answer a question she has asked. Then she has students apply QAR throughout the literacy curriculum. She uses QAR language to ask her students to

* identify the most useful source of information for answering particular questions during guided reading and Read Alouds,

* think about (and record, so they don't forget them) good questions to ask partners when they talk about books,

* justify their answers to In the Book questions by citing specific information in the text that helped them answer the question and sometimes using sticky notes to identify where in the text they found the answer,

* learn that sometimes people can disagree about the best source of information depending on how much they knew about the book or topic beforehand,

* learn that information can be conveyed through both pictures and print, and

* understand that each of us has different experiences that can be combined to answer In My Head questions.

In short, teachers use the two primary-source QARs, In the Book and In My Head, to frame key comprehension strategies (e.g., identifying important information, summarizing, making predictions) for answering questions that probe for high levels of literacy. Students learn how to create questions that push their own and their peers' high-level thinking. Introducing students to the two categories provides a way into talking about where information comes from, the wide range of information sources we draw on to comprehend text, and how information ends up in our heads from these many external sources.

Moving Deeper: Introducing Core QAR Categories

Once students are clear on the two primary sources of information (which, depending on age and experience with QAR can take a few minutes to extended periods of time), the next level, or *core* QARs—Right There, Think & Search, Author & Me, and On My Own—can be introduced in contrasting pairs. Figure 1.4 displays the four core QARs and the pairs that are introduced together.

Notice that QAR instruction always uses paired comparisons. You can introduce students to the two QARs under each source in any order. The paired comparison expanding In the Book focuses students' attention on the difference between Right There and Think & Search QARs. The paired comparison expanding In My Head focuses attention on the difference between Author & Me and On My Own.

Figure 1.4 *The Core Question Answer Relationships*

In the Book QARs

The two In the Book QARs are contrasted to convey the difference between successfully answering a question by simply going to one place in a text and finding all necessary information (Right There) and looking across a text or set of texts to answer the question (Think & Search), as described in Figure 1.5. As shown in Figure 1.7, the Right There QAR fits the NAEP 2009 Framework category called

Locate and Recall. For both fiction and nonfiction texts, this may include answering questions using information explicitly stated in a text source (e.g., magazine, textbook, Web page, chart, or graph) to define a term, providing facts or supporting details. For fiction, it may include identifying information about characters or a setting or determining a sequence of events found in one place in the text. For informational texts, it may include identifying explicitly stated information about topic sentences, determining an author's purpose, explaining a causal relationship, or locating specific information in charts and graphs. Initially, as the definition displayed in Figure 1.5 suggests, for Right There QARs everything needed to answer the question is right there in a single sentence. It's a helpful definition to use initially because it sets up the contrast with Think & Search and leads to analytical thinking.

Think & Search QARs ask readers to put information together from a single text or from a set of texts, looking across sentences, paragraphs, pages, or texts for all the information needed to answer the

Figure 1.5 *In the Book QARs*

In the Book

Right There

The answer is in one place in the text. Words from the question and words that answer the question are often "right there" in the same sentence.

Think & Search

The answer is in the text. Readers need to "think and search," or put together different parts of the text, to find the answer. The answer can be within a paragraph, across paragraphs, or even across chapters and books.

question fully. This fits within the NAEP 2009 Framework category of questions that require students to integrate information, including using multiple text sources to explain the relationships between problems and solutions or causes and effects, providing information about a sequence of events across chapters in a literary text or across chapter sections in an informational text, and comparing or connecting information within and across texts. (See Figure 1.6.)

Figure 1.6 **_NAEP Reading Targets and QAR_**

NAEP Framework Categories	Core QARs
Locate/Recall Identify textually explicit information such as • Definitions • Facts • Supporting details Make simple inferences	**Right There** **Think & Search** • Across small amounts of text, up to several paragraphs
Integrate/Interpret Make complex inferences to • Describe problem and solution, cause and effect • Compare or connect ideas, problems, or situations within or across texts • Determine unstated assumptions in an argument • Analyze how an author uses literary devices and text features	**Think & Search** • Across large amounts of text, including two different texts
Critique/Evaluate Consider text critically to • Judge author's craft and technique • Evaluate the author's perspective or point of view within or across texts • Take different perspectives in relation to a text	**Think & Search** • Usually an examination of the text as a whole • May involve two different texts **Author & Me**

As students become increasingly sophisticated about the range of strategies for locating and identifying relevant information for answering Think & Search questions, we have found that they begin to critique the initial definitions used to distinguish between Think & Search and Right There QARs. Students have made observations such as "This is a Think & Search because I found the information in these two sentences, but they are right next to each other so all I had to do was skim to find the answers. It doesn't seem like it took very much thinking! It seems like this is more like a Right There." You can be proud when your students begin to analyze QARs in this way. An effective way to respond is to turn the observation back to the students, perhaps saying something like "I think Sam has a good point—this does feel like a very simple Think & Search compared to all the others that you are getting so good at answering, using so much text information. Should we just say that if the information is pretty easy to find, all in one place, that it's a Right There? But if you have to look across at least one paragraph and put information together in some way, it's a Think & Search?" When students raise these questions, it indicates that they are becoming reflective about questioning practices, that they have begun to demystify how questions can be created, and that they are learning how comprehension strategies can be used to answer different types of questions effectively. The goal of QAR instruction is to develop students' reflective analysis about questioning, not their ability to simply identify the QAR.

In My Head QARs

The next step in Question Answer Relationships instruction is to introduce the two core In My Head QARs. With both Author & Me and On My Own QARs, as illustrated in Figure 1.7, readers use information from their background knowledge. Neither an Author & Me nor an On My Own question can be answered with only information from the text. You must make clear to students that in order to answer an Author & Me question, readers must have read and understood the text. To answer an On My Own question, readers can rely solely on their background knowledge.

Figure 1.7 *In My Head QARs*

In My Head

On My Own

The answer is not in the text. Readers need to use their own ideas and experiences to answer the question.

Author & Me

The answer is not in the text. To answer the question, readers need to think about how the text and what they already know fit together.

On My Own questions can be used prior to reading a text, to help students access or develop the appropriate background knowledge. When Kathy Highfield's students were about to read Phyllis Reynolds Naylor's novel *Shiloh* (Atheneum, 1991), she asked On My Own questions such as these: "Have you ever had a pet that you cared for? Tell us about it." "Think about people you know who treat their pets especially well. Can you describe their treatment to us?" "Think about people you know or have heard of who may not treat their pets so well. Can you describe the problems these pets have faced?" It wasn't necessary to have read the novel to participate in this discussion.

In contrast, in response to the question "What do you think Marty should have done with Shiloh?" Kathy's students would need to have read the text—to know who Shiloh was, to know why Marty needed to do something with Shiloh, to understand that Marty was going against his parents' wishes. Further, to form a successful answer, they would have to make some complex inferences about the problem Marty faced: His father was worried about his ability to feed another living being, given the family's poverty; Marty's parents were concerned about issues of theft and ownership, since Shiloh had an owner.

Students had to read and understand the text to be able to evaluate Marty's situation. However, no matter how much information from the text they integrate or evaluate, no matter how many times they reread for important information to build their argument, ultimately the source of the answer must come from their background knowledge. Author & Me QARs are defined by this relationship between the text and past experience.

By introducing students to each of the four core categories within the context of two primary information sources—their heads and the text—you can help students avoid confusing the core QARs. If students do not fully understand the two sources, they may confuse Think & Search and Author & Me. They will notice that for both QARs, they have to think about information and use the text. But if they can identify the source, they should be able to identify the appropriate QAR. If the information for the answer comes from their heads, it's an Author & Me QAR. If everything they need can be found in the text(s), then regardless of the question's difficulty, it is a Think & Search QAR.

Sometimes students disagree on the QAR, perhaps arguing strongly that they used their heads, not the book, since they already knew about the topic. Keep in mind that the goal of the QAR framework is for students to be reflective about information sources and about strategies they can use to obtain information. The goal is not simply labeling questions. Since the knowledge held by individuals varies, the emphasis should always be placed on the students' ability to justify their choice of QAR, rather than simply making the same QAR choice as the teacher.

Learning QARs in Context

QAR was designed to be taught and learned in the context of working through a wide range of texts (see, for example, Ezell, Hunsicker, Quinque, & Randolph, 1996). Stephanie Harvey and Anne Goudvis (2000) suggest taking shorter text segments from well-written and interesting material in trade books, magazines, and textbooks and "lifting" them to teach specific instructional strategies. We have used this idea to introduce QARs to students from kindergarten though high school. The length of text lifted depends on the concept being taught. For example, when introducing students to the contrast between In the Book and In My Head, a short paragraph is often enough. To distinguish between Right There and Think & Search in the intermediate grades, usually two to three paragraphs are optimal. A useful guideline for initial text selection—beyond interest and quality of the text—is choosing a section that will fit on a single transparency. This allows you and your students to work through the same passage together and easily see all the text information to which the questions refer.

The text in Figure 1.8 is an example of a lifted passage that can be used in the intermediate grades for various QAR lessons (from Raphael & Au, 2001). It is short enough to fit on a single transparency. The topic is of high interest to intermediate-grade students. The paragraph structure allows you to work with the text in sections or as a whole, depending on what is most appropriate for your students. The content of the passage is sufficiently detailed to invite questions from all four QAR categories and to do so in a way that flows naturally within the cycle of activity

Figure 1.8 *Sample of a Lifted Passage*

Extreme Sports

Can you imagine rocketing down a city street at sixty miles per hour, the speed of a car on the freeway, lying on an overgrown skateboard just inches away from the concrete? How about climbing straight up a frozen waterfall? Or doing a flip on your bike? Or jumping out of an airplane with a snowboard attached to your feet?

Street lugers, ice climbers, BMX freestyle riders, and *sky surfers* are part of the growing world of **extreme sports**.

Just like other athletes, they devote a lot of time to practicing and competing in their sports.

Many of these sports have been created only in the past twenty years. Some sports, like street luging, are all about speed and seeing who can go the fastest. Other sports, like BMX freestyle riding and sky surfing, are about style, or who can do the fanciest stunts. Ice climbing competitors must have both style and speed to win.

before, during, and after reading. (See Chapter 3 for further discussion of QAR and the reading cycle.)

Introducing On My Own QARs

Before reading the passage together, you can raise authentic On My Own QARs by asking students to activate prior knowledge.

On My Own questions for this passage may include

* What are some of your favorite sports?

* What kinds of dangers do you face when you play [fill in the name of the sport]?

* Can you think of any sports that are more dangerous than the ones you have mentioned? What do you think makes this sport extremely dangerous?

As students talk through these questions, it is natural to follow up each discussion with a simple probe, such as "How do you know that?" or "Where did you get the information you used to answer this question?" Research has long shown that comprehension improves when appropriate background knowledge is brought to bear on the reading (Anderson & Pearson, 1984; Hansen & Pearson, 1983; Lipson, 1983). In this lesson you can model the use of background knowledge by asking students to go to their heads as the primary source of information. Note that the information needed to answer any one of these three questions is clearly in the head of the reader, with clues to the source of information for answering the question found in the wording of both the first and the third questions.

In the first question, the choice of wording that asks for "your" favorite sports provides a relatively clear signal that this is an On My Own QAR. This kind of information will not be found in the text. The second question provides a follow up by asking the respondent to consider any dangers in the sport he or she plays, again an On My Own QAR. The words "Can you think of any sports" in question 3 provide a clear signal that the question-asker is seeking information from the reader's own experiences, while the follow-up question "What do you think makes this sport extremely dangerous?" signals that the answerer should be drawing on his or her own experiences to offer an opinion about what makes sports dangerous. An added advantage to using the words "extremely dangerous" in the question is that this introduces vocabulary that is in the selection's title and identifies the types of sports (i.e., dangerous) discussed in the article. As students respond to On My Own QARs, you should help them notice that there are many "right" answers and that the variation in answers can be linked to individual experiences.

Introducing In My Head QARs

You also can use pre-reading discussions to introduce and review the second type of In My Head QAR, Author & Me. Readers usually review texts they are about to read, looking at headers, titles, chapter names, words in bold print, and so forth. For example, asking students "What do you think this article will be about?" is a typical Author & Me question asked prior to reading. Information clearly comes from the reader's head, but a reader needs to sample the text, perhaps noting that "Extreme Sports" appears in bold in two places and that a list of types of sports appears in italics. They may not know what any of this means prior to reading, but they are alerted to the concepts being introduced. In early grades, teachers often engage in a picture walk in which students preview a book by looking at and commenting on the text illustrations. Questions asking them to predict what the text will be about represent Author & Me QARs. The students are using their background knowledge to answer the question (i.e., the "me" in Author & Me), but they know what particular knowledge to use because of information from the text (e.g., headers or illustrations which are the "author" in Author & Me).

The lifted selection about extreme sports presents many opportunities to ask both Right There and Think & Search QARs, in addition to the In My Head QARs discussed above, and to talk about the distinction between the two. For example, after reading the selection, you can present the following pair of questions to students

❋ When were many of these sports created?

* How is the judging of street luging, BMX freestyle riding, and sky surfing similar and different?

It's fairly clear that the answer to the first question involves looking in a single sentence, "Many of these sports have been created only in the past twenty years," while the second question requires some comparing and contrasting over several paragraphs.

Scaffolding QAR Instruction

Teachers have created a range of tools to scaffold their students' thinking about how to respond to different QARs. For example, Jennifer McClorey, a first-grade teacher at Shields Elementary School in Chicago, created a set of flip cards with a primary QAR on each side (i.e., In My Head/In the Book). During a lesson, Jen can distribute the cards so that each student has his or her own card (see Figure 1.9).

When Jen meets with her students for small-group instruction such as guided reading and in whole-class discussions, she is able to see—by the side of the card the students hold up—the source of information

Figure 1.9 *QAR Flip Cards*

students think they are drawing on in response to her questions. The use of the flip card helps in three ways. First, it requires that every student respond to the question. Without this kind of requirement, students may sit back and allow more eager peers to respond, missing an opportunity to apply what they have been learning in the context of discussing text(s). Second, it provides teachers with a general accountability tool—with a quick scan of the room, a teacher can identify students who understand and those who need more help. Third, it gives teachers an opportunity to follow up with students who display a different QAR. In doing so, teachers can remind students that the goal of the instruction is to be able to justify the QAR they have chosen by explaining the information source used, rather than simply choosing what the majority selects as the appropriate QAR.

Figure 1.10 *Poster of Key Words*

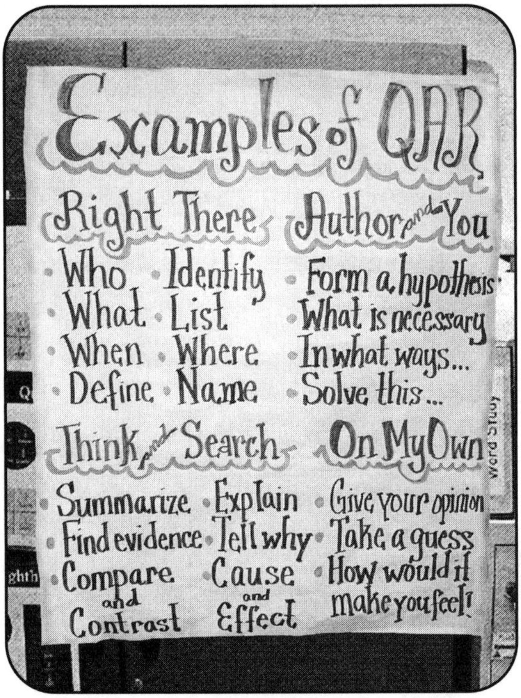

Hannah Natividad, a sixth-grade science teacher at Shields Elementary, has developed a chart of common words associated with the four core QARs when used in the context of answering questions about science texts (see Figure 1.10). However, Hannah makes sure her students understand that these are just guidelines and not hard-and-fast rules. For example, in one circumstance, answering *Who* involves a short Right There search of the text (Who is the scientist responsible for the discovery of . . . ?), while in another it may involve putting together an argument from information in the text (Who has the most reasonable theory for explaining . . . ?). In the former case, students are simply scanning for a particular scientist's name; in the latter, students have to support their response with evidence from several places in the text. In other cases, the QAR is less ambiguous (e.g., Give your opinion . . . , In what ways . . . ?). Hannah's poster provides guidance for her students, helping them link their QAR knowledge to their thinking like scientists. Thus, like all teachers who use QAR, she aims not simply to have her students get the QAR right but, instead, to use QAR language to explore possibilities and, once an answer is constructed, to be able to defend the sources of information chosen to construct it.

Identifying Sources of Difficulty

Taffy described one student who had been very successful in learning about QAR but who was unable to answer one of the questions following reading—he was waving his hand in the air to signal he wanted help. When Taffy went to see if she could help, he responded by saying, "I don't get it." Taffy probed further, asking what he was troubled by in the question. He answered, "I know it's an On My Own, and I went to my head, but there's nothing there." While Taffy was concerned, she also recognized that he was being strategic. He knew that the QAR required that he use his own knowledge to respond well. He attempted to use that knowledge but found he didn't have enough. He knew that if he didn't have what he needed, he must go to an external source for help, and in this case, the appropriate external help was the teacher or other adult in the room (i.e., he wasn't supposed to ask peers for help in this context). In another context, such as preparing for a book discussion or an inquiry project, he may have asked a peer. The important point is that QAR gave him the language with which to pinpoint the specific kind of help he needed, rather than resorting to the vague "I don't get it" that we often hear in classrooms.

Concluding Comments

Teachers we have worked with have found that having the language of QAR helps them in a variety of school contexts. For example, Melissa Tischler teaches middle school language arts at Pulaski School in Chicago. Her students—91 percent of whom qualify for the federal free lunch program—are predominantly Latino, with Spanish as their primary language. In an e-mail (August 27, 2004), she described the importance of QAR to her students' successful book discussions. She noted that prior to teaching them about QAR,

I could not get across the point that some discussion questions did not have right or wrong answers and that not all questions were explicitly answered in the book. As much as I tried to "drill" this . . . , so many of my students kept looking through their novels for answers that were not there. . . . I presented QAR to my class the following week. It was awesome. I will never forget that one of my students looked at me and said, "You're really smart!" [T]he light bulbs finally turned on in their heads and they could think through the differences between In the Book and In My Head.

(e-mail communication, August 27, 2004)

Her success, like that of Janine, Kristin, Tammy, Hannah, and others, suggests that regardless of students' ages or achievement levels, whether used with language arts or across subject areas, QAR provides a solid basis for extensive discussion about strategic thinking; about strategy use in reading, writing, and talking about text; about questioning in everyday classroom activities and on high-stakes tests; and about thinking in and out of school. It provides a language for instruction for students from preschool through high school. In the next chapter, we show you how you can introduce QAR using a six-step lesson format.

Chapter 2

How to Teach QAR Lessons: A Six-Step Model

*I*n her position as an assistant professor of English education at Colorado State University, Pam Coke is helping her students learn to become excellent classroom teachers. She wants them to have first-hand experience with the strategies they will be teaching to their students. In a recent e-mail to Taffy Raphael, she wrote

> We are trying to practice as many strategies as we can, as we read, discuss, and engage with texts this semester, so I asked students to practice four types of questions [QARs] with the next chapter of the text. They were adept at creating "right there" questions. They felt fairly comfortable with "pulling it together" questions, though they felt this type of question started to blur with the "author and
>
> *(continued on next page)*

me" questions. They were completely stymied by "author and me" and "on my own" questions. My question for you is this: Do you have any strategies or references you would recommend to me to help students understand how to write and use these kinds of questions in the classroom?

(e-mail communication September 12, 2005)

Pam is requesting the information that is central to the focus of this chapter. Once we—teachers and teacher educators—understand the language and definitions of the four QAR categories, we need effective ways to teach them to our students. In the last chapter we provided background about QAR—its underlying rationale, the four QAR categories, and some of the ways QAR aligns with comprehension instruction. This chapter addresses the next logical question: how should we teach lessons on QARs? We begin by focusing on the theoretical basis from which we developed the model for QAR instruction. Then we describe a six-step model for lessons that can provide high-quality QAR instruction for all students.

Sociocultural Theory and QAR Instruction

The ideas of the Russian psychologist Lev Vygotsky form the basis for sociocultural theory, which emphasizes the importance of the social world in human development and learning. According to Vygotsky (1981, 1986) and later sociocultural theorists, it is through social interactions that higher mental or psychological processes, such as language and literacy learning, occur. Learning does not take place within the individual as a process of maturation alone. For example, when a parent repeats the word *juice* as she or he hands a toddler a cup of juice, the parent models appropriate language use. The toddler tries to say what he or she has just heard, but says "juh" instead of "juice." The parent elaborates on the child's efforts, saying, "Juice. You want some *juice*. Can you say *juice?*" Eventually, the child will be able to ask for juice, without scaffolding from the adult. Through support and encouragement from a "more capable other," the child gradually learns to speak.

In the classroom, we follow this same model to teach students about QARs and/or other forms of higher-level thinking. We describe the different types of QARs and model and demonstrate their use. We then assist students as they attempt to use QARs for themselves. In the beginning, we know that we will probably have to give students considerable assistance. Over time, students will gain the ability to use QARs more and more independently. This is the idea of the gradual release of responsibility, as shown in Figure 2.1.

Figure 2.1 *Gradual Release of Responsibility*

Gradual Release of Responsibility

- Explicit Explanation
- Modeling
- Guided Practice
- Coaching
- Independent Application
- Self-Assessment and Goal Setting

High Teacher Control
Low Student Activity

Low Teacher Control
High Student Activity

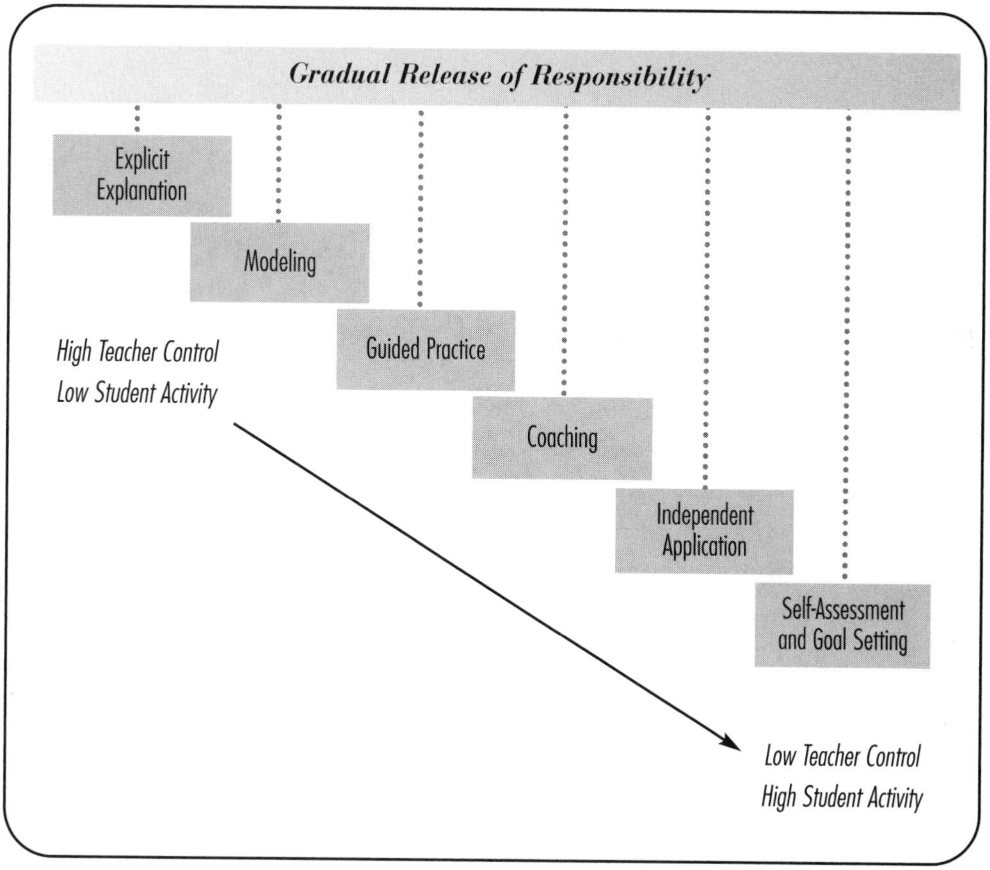

Figure 2.2 *The Vygotsky Space*

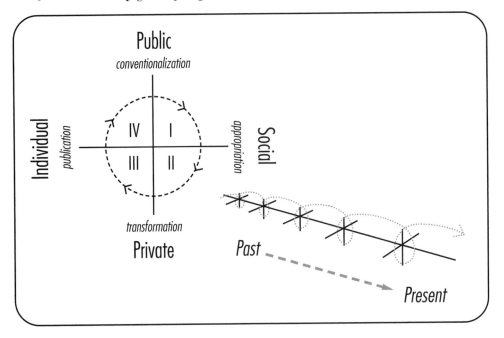

The Vygotsky Space and QAR Instruction

In Chapter 1 we emphasized that there is more to QAR instruction than teaching students the four categories of On My Own, Author & Me, Right There, and Think & Search and having them give the right answers. The larger purpose of QAR instruction is to improve reading comprehension by giving students a language to talk about sources of information and their thinking about text. Sociocultural theory, and specifically the concept known as the Vygotsky Space (Harré, 1984), can help us understand how we can provide QAR instruction to accomplish this.

The Vygotsky Space (see Figure 2.2) is a rich concept that explains how particular kinds of teacher-student talk in a range of settings enable students to learn complex ideas. We'll walk through its components, step by step.

Figure 2.2 illustrates the process Vygotsky was describing when he wrote that all learning is situated in the social and public spaces in which we interact with more capable others. The vertical axis represents the transition from public to private talk, thought, and action. How does this work in the classroom? Imagine you are explicitly describing the difference between In the Book and In My Head. This is public, for all students to see and hear. At the other end of the axis are students' private thoughts—we are unable to access these unless we ask students to leave a trace. We may ask for a written product or listen in on a conversation or even record it on audiotape for later reflection on what they have learned.

The horizontal axis represents the range of an individual's strategy use or concept understanding. On one side is the socially accepted or conventional use or understanding. On the other end is innovative or transformed use. For example, QARs might be conventionally described as the relationship between the question asked and the source of information used for answering it. However, Jennifer McClorey and her first-grade students transformed the description of QAR to "how questions and answers get along." That description's meaning in their classroom developed from extensive interactions involving both public interaction and socially accepted definitions.

Understanding the Four Quadrants of the Vygotsky Space

The two axes form quadrants, or spaces, that help us see how ideas that are initially in the public and social space of the classroom can be adapted and/or transformed by students and teachers alike. Further, the diagram illustrates how socially accepted or conventional ideas can be changed over time by the input of people who are working with them. Four processes mark movement from one quadrant to the next:

* appropriation
* transformation
* publication
* conventionalization

Let us go through each quadrant of the learning cycle and the processes that define movement through the cycle, using QAR as an example.

Quadrant I: Public-Social

Quadrant I, the public-social space, typically starts the learning cycle. The activity in this space is designed to make thinking about QAR

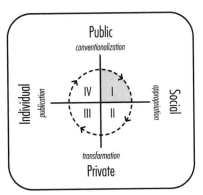

visible to students. Typical instruction includes teachers modeling, thinking aloud, and demonstrating. That instruction is part of the public-social context for learning, in which all students can have access to new information. As an example of this, later in this chapter you will see a third-grade teacher give a lesson on the difference between On My Own and Author & Me, the two In My Head QARs.

When moving from Quadrant I to Quadrant II, students have the opportunity to engage in the process of *appropriation*—the shift of knowledge from the public arena into the individual's own thoughts. In the lesson you'll see later, students begin to learn about On My Own and Author & Me by appropriating, or picking up, knowledge of the difference between these two QARs as explained and modeled by the teacher.

Quadrant II: Private-Social

Quadrant II is the private-social area. Here students have the opportunity to understand for themselves the new knowledge made

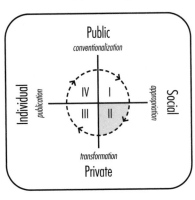

available by the teacher. They practice using it independently, following the teacher's modeling. For example, in the lesson we describe later, the teacher has the students read a text together and generate On My Own and Author & Me questions. Then the teacher has the students go through the same task while working with partners. Students are thinking about QAR individually, but all their efforts take place as part of a whole-class lesson under the teacher's guidance and then in partner work with teacher coaching. In this way, their learning is private (i.e., engaged in independently) but put to use in the socially conventional way in which they were taught.

Quadrant III: Private-Individual

In contrast to Quadrant II's emphasis on using a skill conventionally—just as it was taught—Quadrant III, the private-individual area,

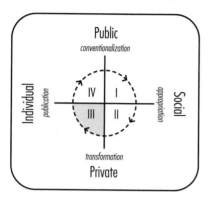

emphasizes the process of *transformation*. Students work without the support of the "more capable other" to transform the ideas to make them their own. Students work on their own, and their work reflects innovative thinking— individualized ways of taking what they have learned in new and effective directions. In the QAR classroom described later, the teacher has students work individually. She assigns a paragraph of the text and asks students to generate On My Own and Author & Me questions. Students must read and write questions for themselves, questions that fit the two categories they have been studying, without coaching from the teacher or assistance from a peer. Successful students do not simply repeat questions, using the patterns they have learned; they use what they have learned in innovative ways.

Quadrant IV: Public-Individual

In moving to Quadrant IV, students make public what they have learned. In our example, the teacher has the class come back as a whole group so

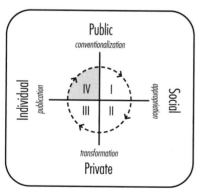

that the students can share their questions and answers and discover new patterns of questions and innovative strategies for answering them. In this public situation, students have the opportunity to demonstrate their grasp of QAR and their own individual ways of interpreting how this knowledge can be used. The teacher has the chance to assess their learning and provide them with feedback and assistance as needed. Students also assess their own learning. For example, in Chapter 1 we introduced students who critiqued the definition of a Think & Search QAR. They suggested that if the information is found in adjacent sentences or within a single small paragraph, it should be called a Right There QAR. Their comments reflected individual ways of thinking, and by making their innovative thinking public, they transformed how their classroom distinguished Right There from Think & Search.

Adoption of innovations such as refining the definition of a Right There or creating a new symbol for clarification questions is central to the process called *conventionalization*. New ideas can become accepted conventions. Conventionalization is a significant part of the learning process—it indicates that students have a deep understanding of the concept and shows that they will be able to apply their understanding in ways that were not explicitly taught.

A Classroom Climate That Encourages Innovation

To help students gain a deep understanding of concepts, teachers must establish a climate in which risk taking and questioning conventional ways of doing things are valued. For example, Laura Pardo, a fifth-grade teacher in Lansing, Michigan, encouraged her students to experiment with creating new patterns of questioning. This had a powerful impact. Not only did students learn to value one another's innovations, but they also began to engage in the act of innovation. To help her students prepare for interesting book club discussions—small, student-led discussion groups—she taught them the importance of asking Author & Me questions. Students invented patterns of questions that fit this category and that they believed would contribute to interesting discussions. Students created a "Me and the Book" QAR, in which they could think about what they themselves would do in a similar situation. They created an "In the Characters' Shoes" QAR, in which peers had to consider what they would do if they were in the characters' situation. Students would be unlikely to engage in this level of thinking while responding to reading if the classroom climate did not encourage innovation.

The Cycle of Learning and the Vygotsky Space

Returning to the Vygotsky Space (see Figure 2.2), notice the circle again. This circle represents one cycle of learning that learners of all ages may go through when learning a new higher-level mental process. For example, Taffy Raphael (1986) describes how a group of teachers had read about QAR and discussed the four core categories in what Vygotsky would consider Quadrant I, the public and social space. They talked in a faculty meeting about the conventional way in which QAR is defined and made recommendations for teaching QAR. Then the teachers, engaging in the process of appropriation, moved from Quadrant I to Quadrant II, applying what they had learned as they taught QAR to their own students, using the conventional terminology (e.g., Right There, Think & Search). However, one teacher moved almost immediately from Quadrant II to Quadrant III, through a process of transformation, discovering that her students grasped Think & Search more easily if they used the phrase "putting it together" instead. In that sense, she had moved to the private (i.e., her own thinking) and individual (i.e., her transformed way of teaching QAR) space. No one knew about this transformation until she made it public informally, in conversation with others at her school, then more formally at another faculty meeting—a step that marked her movement into Quadrant IV. Other teachers liked this idea, so in this school, Putting It Together became the accepted, or conventional, term for Think & Search QARs.

This cycle may occur within a single lesson, across a set of lessons, or across a student's school career. The lower right part of Figure 2.2 illustrates this temporal dimension of learning. We don't simply revisit earlier ideas—we are constantly in a process of appropriating and transforming what we have learned, making our learning public and contributing to what becomes conventional knowledge. Thus, the spiral movement from past to present represents the ongoing development of an individual student's higher-level mental processes associated with QAR and reading comprehension. It can also represent the ongoing development of the classroom as a discourse community in which all students are supported in acquiring and using with increasing sophistication the language to discuss QAR and reading comprehension. Creating this kind of learning community, in which all students are supported, directly addresses concerns about equity raised in Chapter 1.

A Six-Step Instructional Model

The processes central to learning as described in the Vygotsky model underscore the importance of specific kinds of teacher talk, teacher-student talk, and student-student interactions. Researchers (e.g., Brown, Campione, & Day, 1981; Pearson, 1985; Rodgers, 1995; Wood, Bruner, & Ross, 1976) have characterized support for children's learning in terms of scaffolded instruction—providing temporary and adjustable support for what students are as yet unable to do independently. Kathryn Au and Taffy Raphael (1998) created a model of such instruction in a balanced literacy curriculum, showing the gradual release of responsibility from more teacher control and less student activity to less teacher control and more student activity. The six steps in the instructional model for teaching QAR derive from several of these sources.

In the instructional model for teaching QAR lessons presented here, we use a text typical of the ones students read for social studies in third grade, often referred to as a "pseudo-narrative" because it conveys content information through a story. We describe how Ms. Jones (a composite of many effective teachers we have observed teaching QAR) might go about planning and conducting a QAR lesson based on this social studies text. As we mentioned in Chapter 1, many teachers find it convenient to teach QAR lessons with excerpts from texts that students are reading as part of the ongoing classroom curriculum. In our example, Ms. Jones has chosen to use a passage lifted from "Qillak" (from Raphael & Au, 2001). This text describes how an Inuit boy went about building his own kayak.

Ms. Jones chose the passage from "Qillak" for two reasons. First, she felt that it was a straightforward text that most students in her class would understand. Second, she wanted to use a social studies text to show students that QARs could be used during the reading of content area material, as well as in reading or language arts. Ms. Jones had already introduced the primary QAR categories of In My Head and In the Book during the language arts period. However, research suggests that students tend to associate strategies only with the contexts in which they have been taught (Duke & Pearson, 2002; Singer & Donlan, 1982). Ms. Jones wanted her students to both appropriate and transform QAR in the course of reading a variety of texts throughout the day, so she knew it was important not to confine QAR lessons to the language arts period. Here is her six-step lesson.

1. Explicit explanation

The first step in the instructional model is explicit explanation, the kind of public, social talk that is typical of Quadrant I of the Vygotsky Space. In this step, the teacher makes sure that students know exactly what they are going to learn about using QARs: the specific language of QAR and how QAR can help them become good readers. Many teachers connect their QAR lessons to state standards, grade-level benchmarks, and student-friendly I Can statements. (We describe this further in Chapter 6 (Au, 2006; Au, Hirata, & Raphael, 2005).) In our example, Ms. Jones begins the QAR lesson by saying the following to her students:

> It's time for our social studies lesson now, and we're doing something a little different today. Today's lesson will help you with a very important I Can statement posted on our bulletin board: I can generate and respond to questions based on fiction and nonfiction texts. Asking and answering questions is one way to improve your reading comprehension or understanding of what you're reading.
>
> Let me explain why I planned this lesson. Yesterday during language arts time, I taught you about Question Answer Relationships, or QAR. Who remembers what we said about the two sources of information you could use to answer questions? That's right, In My Head and In the Book, just as it says on the chart we made yesterday. Today I'm going to teach you that In My Head actually involves two different kinds of QARs. Knowing these two new QARs will help to improve your reading comprehension. I also want you to understand that you don't use QAR only during reading in language arts. You should use QAR whenever you read, including during social studies.

Now here are the two kinds of In My Head QARs. The first kind is On My Own. The answer to an On My Own question has to come from what you already know. You can't find the answer anywhere in the text. The second kind is Author & Me. To answer an Author & Me question, you have to use your own knowledge to answer the question, but you'll know which knowledge to use only if you have read and understood the text. The text helps you figure out what, of all the things you know, you will want to use to answer the question.

Note that Ms. Jones stated the purpose of the lesson and connected it to an I Can statement. She and the other third-grade teachers had developed this I Can statement to align with the state content standard for reading comprehension. Ms. Jones made the connection to what the students had learned about QAR during the language arts period and let them know that they would be learning more about QAR and that they should apply what they have learned about QAR during social studies and other subject areas.

2. Modeling

After setting the purpose for the lesson through explicit explanation, the teacher moves on to modeling, or demonstrating QAR application in interactions typical of Quadrant I. During modeling the teacher shows students how to carry out the strategy. Reading comprehension is an invisible mental process, but modeling makes it visible. Teachers often use Think Alouds for this purpose (Schunk & Zimmerman, 1997). During a Think Aloud, the teacher verbalizes the thoughts that go through the mind of a proficient reader who is working to comprehend a text. In this case, she says aloud her thoughts and generates questions. Using an overhead transparency or chart of the lifted passage, the teacher points to the sentences as she reads the passage aloud. She stops along the way to verbalize her thoughts about the passage.

Ms. Jones introduced the Think Aloud by telling students she would be reading to understand the text, and then she would go back through the text to generate On My Own and Author & Me questions. Here is the Think Aloud that Ms. Jones did for the first two paragraphs of "Qillak."

The people of the arctic lands of North America are Inuit. (*Arctic lands, I know something about that. Inuit. I've heard that term but I wasn't sure what it meant.*) Long ago, they lived off the sea and hunted seals and walruses in boats call kayaks. (*I see people using kayaks on the lake but I never thought about using kayaks for hunting. I think it would be hard to hunt from a kayak.*)

For two years, Qillak watched his older brother paddle out to sea. His brother would go and hunt with his father and the men of the village. (*So Qillak has an older brother. That reminds me of my older sister. I always wanted to be able to do what my older sister did.*) Qillak dreamed of the day when he would hunt for seals. In a few months, he would be old enough. (*Just as I thought, he can't wait to grow up.*) Qillak thought about that day, and he grew more excited as it got nearer the time.

Qillak had watched the men and older boys in his village build their kayaks since he was a little boy. (*I've seen kayaks but I've never watched anyone build a kayak.*) Now the time had come for him to build his own kayak. (*Qillak knows more than I do. I wouldn't know the first thing about building a kayak.*)

Then Ms. Jones started a T-chart titled "In My Head QARs." She labeled the two columns on the T-chart "On My Own" and "Author & Me." She told the class:

Now that I've finished reading these three paragraphs, I want to generate an On My Own question. Let me reread from the beginning. "The people of the arctic lands of North America are Inuit." Oh, good, I have an idea from the very first sentence: What do you know about the arctic lands? This is a good On My Own question because these paragraphs don't tell me anything about the arctic lands, and it helps to know about the arctic lands to understand where Qillak is living. If others can share what they know with me, it will help me make more sense of this story.

Ms. Jones wrote her question in the "On My Own" column. She continued:

> Now for an Author & Me question. Let me reread the second paragraph. "For two years, Qillak watched his older brother paddle out to sea." Reading about Qillak and his brother made me think about my older sister and me. I think I'll generate a question about Qillak and how his family might compare with mine: How might Qillak's family be similar to and different from your family? This is a good Author & Me question because to answer you have to combine what you learned from reading about Qillak's family with knowledge of your own family.

Ms. Jones wrote this question under the heading "Author & Me." As the lesson continued, Ms. Jones added student-generated questions to the chart, too.

During the Think Aloud, Ms. Jones modeled for students how a good reader thinks actively about the text in order to generate questions. Some teachers hesitate to model with Think Alouds because they feel the comments they make must be profound or insightful. This concern is ungrounded. Simply sharing the ordinary thoughts that come to mind, as Ms. Jones did, is very effective.

3. Guided practice

After students have seen the strategy modeled, they are ready to try using it under the teacher's guidance, while remaining with the whole group. This kind of activity represents the beginning of the transition to Quadrants II and III. During guided practice, the teacher has students try out the strategy, but with the scaffolding they need to appropriate and transform it to achieve their goals. Ms. Jones continued the lesson:

> *Now let's see if we can work together to ask some On My Own questions. Here's a hint. What I did was look for something that seems important, like arctic lands, but isn't really discussed in the text. Let's go back to the first paragraph and read the second sentence together: "Long ago, they lived off the sea and hunted seals and walruses in boats called kayaks." Can anyone think of an On My Own question based on this sentence?*

Several students raised their hands. One student suggested asking a question about kayaks, such as "How can kayaks be used?" Ms. Jones had the student explain why this was a good On My Own question and then added this and other questions suggested by students to the chart.

Next, Ms. Jones asked the students to try to generate Author & Me questions. She suggested that they try the approach she had used earlier. "I took something from the text, such as Qillak's older brother, and I thought about how I could make a connection to it, so that the answer to the question comes from my head. That was how I made an

---

One Caution

Teachers should be alert to the difference between *showing* students what to do and *telling* them what to do. For example, Ms. Jones showed the students that to generate questions, she reread the text. She sent students a more convincing message by actually demonstrating rereading rather than by just telling students to reread. Research by Barbara Taylor and her colleagues (Taylor, Peterson, Pearson, & Rodriguez, 2002) underscores the important difference between demonstrating and telling. Modeling and coaching encourage higher levels of thinking, while telling and recitation reinforce lower levels of thinking. Many students will go quickly through the text once and not return to it for closer study. Ms. Jones modeled the thoughtful rereading and analysis required by readers of all levels to generate useful On My Own, Author & Me, and other questions.

Author & Me question." She suggested that students start with the idea of Qillak's dream of hunting. A student came up with the question, "What is your dream?" Ms. Jones commented that this was a good question but pointed out that it was an On My Own because it could be answered without reading the text. She added the question to the chart under "On My Own" and then asked if anyone could ask a question that brought in Qillak's dream but included an opinion. A student suggested: "Do you think Qillak's dream will come true?" Ms. Jones helped the student to explain why this was a good Author & Me question: It mentioned Qillak's dream, which a reader would know only if he or she read the text, but asked the reader to make a prediction, which could come only from the reader's head. Ms. Jones suggested adding "Why or why not?" to the question, so that the answer would go beyond a simple yes or no. Notice that the teacher encouraged students not only to develop and refine their questions but also to articulate the reason for classifying the question as On My Own or Author & Me. You should be prepared to accept a range of question possibilities, provided that students are able to back up their choices with a strong rationale.

4. Coaching

In the fourth step, coaching, students apply what they have learned about QARs as they work on tasks with a partner or as part of a small group, typical of activities within Quadrants II and III. Because students have help from their peers, the teacher is able to circulate, monitoring student progress and providing assistance as needed. Further, listening to students share with peers offers teachers a window into their thinking. Coaching involves the teacher in scaffolding student performance, usually through cueing.

Ms. Jones set up this part of the lesson by saying the following:

We worked together as a class to generate On My Own and Author &
Me questions. Now you're going to work with a partner to think of one
question in each category. Read and discuss the next paragraph together.
Then think of one On My Own and one Author & Me question.

Here is the paragraph students were asked to read:

> First, Qillak had to build a wooden frame. Not many trees grow in the arctic fields, so Qillak walked along the seashore looking for driftwood. After four weeks of looking, he had collected enough wood to build the wooden frame. Qillak used tools made of sharp stones to shape the wood into the frame for his kayak.

Ms. Jones walked around the classroom, listening to the conversations occurring between partners, with particular attention to pairs of students who seemed to be struggling to create their questions. She talked with them to determine the source or sources of their problem, and then she offered coaching by giving them cues. For example, she noticed one pair of students who appeared to be stuck in their efforts to generate a question, with no idea of where to begin. They said they had read everything through and now could not remember what to ask about. Because they were not looking back in the text, she suggested, "Remember to reread each sentence carefully so you can get ideas about possible questions." A second pair of students showed her questions they had created, and she noticed that the questions were In the Book, testlike questions rather than more engaging questions that solicited links to their background knowledge. She reminded them that they were working to create On My Own and Author & Me questions, then prompted them to think about asking for information not found in the text. "Can you think of something important to know about Qillak, the arctic, or kayaks that isn't discussed much in the text?" A third pair of students had their hands raised. They explained that they wanted to ask about kayaks but that most of their friends have never built one. To this pair, she noted, "It's true that most people don't build kayaks, but people build a lot of other things. Can you think of a question that would help someone make a connection to what Qillak is doing?"

Ms. Jones supplied cues but left responsibility for coming up with the actual questions to students. This is an important feature of coaching. Students must do the bulk of the cognitive work. Notice that Ms. Jones did not simply tell students what to write (e.g., telling the third pair "Write a question that asks about something someone in the class has built"). Further, while students are working in pairs or small groups, the teacher has the opportunity to customize assistance and respond to specific questions in ways that are not possible with the whole group. In the examples above, each pair was struggling with a different problem/issue, and Ms. Jones was able to adjust the temporary supports needed for each situation.

When the pairs had finished their work, Ms. Jones called the class back together. In activities typical of Quadrant IV, she encouraged them to appropriate and transform their ideas by sharing their responses and to provide reasons for their choices. She then added the questions students had generated to the chart.

5. Independent application

During independent application, students attempt to carry out the targeted comprehension strategy (i.e., generating Author & Me and On My Own QARs) on their own, an activity typical of Quadrants II and III. To set up the independent-application phase of the lesson, Ms. Jones told students:

> You and your partners did a good job of asking On My Own and Author & Me questions. Now it's time to see how well you can ask these two kinds of questions on your own. Read the next paragraph and see if you can think of one On My Own question and one Author & Me question. I'm going to ask why you think each of those questions is an On My Own or an Author & Me, so be ready to give me a good reason.

The following is the paragraph students read for this part of the lesson.

Coaching: The Neglected Step

In our observations, coaching appears to be the step most often neglected, especially in the reading instruction of students of diverse backgrounds. In many reading programs, lessons skip from guided practice with the whole class straight to independent application. This poses a problem, especially for struggling readers who need the additional scaffolding provided by coaching. Our model allows this scaffolded help to come from both peers and the teacher.

QAR Now: Question Answer Relationships

> Soon, Qillak was ready to put the pieces of the frame together. He had collected and dried the guts of seals that men in the village had hunted. He used the dried guts to tie the pieces of wood together. Qillak's brother helped him by holding the pieces of wood together, and soon Qillak's wooden frame was finished.

To make students' progress more easily visible to her, Ms. Jones distributed a T-chart to each student, similar to the one they had used at the opening of the lesson. The page was divided into two columns, with "Author & Me" and "On My Own" as the two column headers. Ms. Jones gathered assessment information by observing the students as they worked to list an appropriate question in each column of the chart.

She did not provide coaching at this time, except to two struggling readers, because she wanted to see what students could do on their own. She jotted down the names of the two struggling readers as well as other students who seemed to be experiencing difficulty so that she could be sure to provide them with additional scaffolding in future QAR lessons. For example, during guided reading with these two students, she planned to emphasize the types of questions she was asking as well as to prompt them to create a question of each type to ask their peers during the lesson. She also planned some at-home practice with a series of short paragraphs from their upcoming social studies text. This practice served a dual purpose: (1) it gave them the opportunity to practice reading the text before the class did, and (2) it provided them with practice in generating comprehension questions that she could feature during in-class discussions—making the practice more meaningful to them. If they needed additional work, she planned in the future to ask them to look at questions that were part of the end-of-chapter activities in their textbook and classify them by QAR type.

6. Self-assessment and goal setting

When students have completed the assignment, the teacher calls the whole class together for a discussion. In Ms. Jones's class, students shared the questions they had generated, and she had them explain why

Figure 2.3 *In My Head Questions T-chart*

On My Own	Author & Me
What do you know about the arctic lands?	How might Qillak's family be similar to and different from your family?
What would you do if you had a kayak?	Do you think Qillak's dream will come true? Why or why not?
What is your dream?	Discuss a time when you used tools and compare that to Qillak's use of tools.
What is driftwood?	How is where you live different from where Qillak lives?
What are some different uses for a wooden frame?	Do you think Qillak could have built the kayak by himself? Why or why not?
What are some ways brothers and sisters help each other?	What would you like about Qillak's way of life? What would you not like?

each was an On My Own or an Author & Me. After they had shared this information, she had them look at all the On My Own questions in the chart (see Figure 2.3) and describe what they noticed.

Students noticed, for example, that many of the questions required the reader to think about his or her own life and that the reader had to know vocabulary, such as *arctic* and *driftwood*. She guided the students through a parallel analysis of all the Author & Me questions. One student noticed that several questions required comparing yourself to the person in the text, and another student observed that two questions included the phrase "why or why not."

After the discussion, Ms. Jones referred students back to the I Can statement "I can generate and respond to questions based on fiction and nonfiction texts." She handed out the self-assessment forms, with which students were already familiar (see Figure 2.4).

She told students the following:

Now it's time for self-assessment. Start by copying the I Can statement onto your self-assessment form. Then write at least one thing you learned from today's lesson. If you have learned more than one thing, please write down those, too. When you have thought about all you have learned, think about anything that confused you. If you have any ideas for what kind of help you want, write about that. Think about what kind of help might be most useful—more practice with a partner or small group? Hearing me talk about the two kinds of QAR with a new text? Practice writing questions on your own? Sharing questions with the class? This will help me figure out what I can do to help you. Also remember to rate your participation and include reasons for your rating.

Notice that Ms. Jones did not mention QAR, On My Own, or Author & Me at this point because she wanted to see if students would use any of these terms of their own accord. Nor did she mention anything about Qillak, for the same reason.

From the brief discussion that followed, and from reading students' T-charts and self-assessments, Ms. Jones discovered that most of them understood how to generate On My Own questions but wanted more help with Author & Me questions. Several students wrote that they liked working with partners and found it harder to generate questions when they were working alone. This information helped Ms. Jones know that she should reteach the Author & Me category before going on to the two In the Book QARs, Right There and Think & Search. Ms. Jones verified that students benefited from partner work, and she decided that more partner work might give

Name: Nick   Date: 2/1/06

I Can Statement:
I can write and respond to questions based on fiction and nonfiction texts.

What I learned:
I learned how to write On My Own questions.

What I don't understand or need help with:
I need more help with Author and Me questions.

What would help me:
More practice

Rating of my participation in the lesson:

Excellent   (Good)   Needed Improvement

Reason for this rating:
I made up two questions.

Teacher comments:

Sample of a completed self-assessment form

Figure 2.4 *Student Self-Assessment Form*

Name: Date:

I Can Statement:

What I learned:

What I don't understand or need help with:

What would help me:

Rating of my participation in the lesson:

Excellent   Good   Needed Improvement

Reason for this rating:

Teacher comments:

QAR Now: Question Answer Relationships

Guidelines for Developing QAR Lessons

Following these guidelines will increase the opportunities for literacy learning, especially for students of diverse backgrounds.

1. Begin QAR instruction as soon as possible in the school year. This will maximize the opportunities for students to benefit from it.

2. Follow all six steps in the model. Be sure to include coaching.

3. Provide consistent, repeated instruction.

4. Increase students' engagement by having them collaborate. Provide opportunities for them to work in groups and with partners.

students the scaffolding they needed to progress to generating questions independently.

Throughout the lesson, Ms. Jones used the language of QAR so that students would learn terms and concepts such as On My Own, Author & Me, generating questions, and giving reasons for answers. Students listened to Ms. Jones and then were required to use the same language and concepts themselves during whole-class discussions, when working with a partner, when seeking individual help from Ms. Jones, and when writing to complete their self-assessment forms. As the sample lesson shows, QAR instruction and learning how to engage in higher-level thinking with text form an ongoing process in the classrooms of effective teachers. Students and teachers need a common language for discussing comprehension of text and the difficulties encountered with comprehension. QAR provides such a language. Once this language is in place, students can explain what they understand and do not understand, and teachers can better plan instruction to help students progress to the next level. Figure 2.5 provides a guide for lesson planning that can be applied to any grade level or subject area.

Figure 2.5 *Six-Step Model Lesson Planning Guide*

Subject: Date:

Goals for Student Learning

Standard:

Benchmark:

I Can Statement:

QAR Focus:

Materials Needed

 Text:

 Other Materials (such as self-assessment forms):

Six Steps in Lesson

Step 1—Explicit Explanation	**Step 4—Coaching**
Notes: What to say to students about the purpose of the lesson	Part of text to be used: Notes: Grouping (partner or small group), instructions for students, possible cues
Step 2—Modeling Part of text to be used: Notes: Think aloud and modeling of QAR focus	**Step 5—Independent Application** Part of text to be used: Notes: Instructions for students, students to monitor
Step 3—Guided Practice Part of text to be used: Notes: Possible questions, examples	**Step 6—Self-Assessment & Goal Setting** Notes: Instructions for students

Concluding Comments

We hope you view the sample lesson in this chapter as a source of ideas that you can adapt for use in your own classroom. For example, you may want to develop your own I Can statements based on state standards for reading comprehension, perhaps having students discuss the wording that makes the I Can statements clear to them (see Chapter 6). Or you may want to experiment with having students work in groups of three, rather than in pairs. Or you may want to redesign the form that students use for self-assessment. Ideas in the sample lesson, such as tips for doing effective Think Alouds, could be developed further as part of teacher study groups, as discussed in Chapter 7. In the next chapter we explore how QAR can be used as a framework for comprehension instruction.

Chapter 3

How QAR Frames
Comprehension Instruction

*W*hile participating in an inquiry project at the University of
Illinois at Chicago, Leah Werab, a fifth-grade teacher at Oscar
Mayer Elementary, a fine arts magnet school in Chicago, described a
realization she had about higher-order thinking:

> I realized quickly after beginning teaching that I needed a
> language and a way to teach students about higher-order thinking
> that they could easily understand and apply to their work.

Leah was concerned that students not only were unaware of
different types of questions and related task demands but also "lacked
the ability to describe their thoughts with regard to questions and had

different vocabulary based on which classroom they were in the previous year." In short, Leah, like many teachers, was concerned about the lack of a coherent comprehension curriculum—one that would allow her to build upon the previous year and effectively prepare her students for the demands of the next year. She believed that "introducing them to QAR helped to relieve some of these problems."

In Chapters 1 and 2, we introduced QAR and showed how the different types of QARs can be introduced to students with a six-step lesson. In this chapter, we explore how QAR can help frame comprehension instruction by giving you a way to organize your instruction and build upon previous lessons—from earlier grade levels as well as earlier in the year. First, we describe the reading cycle and how QAR can make visible the types of questions often asked and answered within each phase of the cycle (before, during, and after reading). Then we illustrate how comprehension strategies align with specific QARs. Finally, we show how you can move from explicitly instructing students about QAR, as described in Chapter 2, to using it as a language to communicate about comprehension strategies and instruction.

Helping Students See How Comprehension Strategies Relate

There are many well-documented and extensively researched strategies and skills that enhance students' comprehension and higher-level thinking in response to text. There is also extensive research showing that comprehension strategies and skills can be taught (Pearson & Fielding, 1991; Pressley, 2002; Raphael & Brock, 1997; Snow, 2003). This knowledge base about comprehension strategies and instruction is both a blessing and a curse. Clearly, it's a blessing for readers to have a large repertoire of strategies and skills to draw upon as they encounter texts from a variety of genres. But the extensive number of strategies and their range of applicable contexts can be a curse for the teacher who must organize them for instruction and for the student who must figure out the relationships between all the strategies learned.

Students have to understand more than just the individual strategies themselves. They must learn

* how strategies work together;

* that there are multiple strategies that may be appropriate at different points in the reading cycle; and

* that they need to develop—over the course of the school year and as they progress to higher grade levels—a growing sophistication for applying strategies to increasingly difficult texts for increasingly challenging purposes.

Teachers have access to a range of resources to determine which comprehension skills and strategies to teach at their grade levels. They may consult scope-and-sequence guides that accompany commercially produced reading programs. Their state department of education Web sites may describe strategies to help students achieve particular benchmarks. They may turn to professional journals for research-based strategies to teach (e.g., summarizing, predicting, visualizing). Often though, teachers are overwhelmed by the sheer number of strategies and the lack of a conceptual framework or model to help their students (and the teachers themselves) see the relationships among the strategies.

Embedding QAR Language Within the Reading Cycle

Capable readers understand that the kinds of thinking they engage in and the related questions they ask as they read vary depending on where they are in the reading cycle—before, during, or after reading the text. For example, prior to reading, we are more likely to invoke background knowledge about the author, the genre, and the content of the text. During reading, we make connections between textual ideas, identify information that is important, and visualize text events or processes. After we have read, we connect ideas to broader themes and engage in reflections that invoke text-to-self connections. Thus, the types of questions we ask ourselves or ask our students are not uniform across the reading cycle. It's important for students to understand this variation, and QAR provides a language to talk about it (see Figure 3.1).

Before reading, students are most likely to encounter In My Head questions, designed to prompt them to think about relevant prior knowledge. These, of course, include both On My Own questions, which ask for information that is not found in the text, and Author & Me questions, which may require some minimal information from and interaction with the text, such as a look at the table of contents, chapter titles, pictures, or book-jacket information.

During reading, the QARs students most frequently encounter are designed to help them identify important information (Right There or Think & Search), synthesize or integrate information from the text (Think & Search), and interpret information from the text in light of their own experience (Author & Me).

Figure 3.1 ***Flow of QAR Through the Reading Cycle***

After reading, most QARs are (or should be) Author & Me or Think & Search, as readers make text-to-self connections, link what they have read to overarching themes and issues, and connect across sets of related texts.

QAR and the Reading Cycle: In Action in the Classroom

A look into Maria Ruiz Blanco's third-grade classroom in Belmont-Cragin School, in Chicago, during one language arts period illustrates how the QARs vary before, during, and after reading a text. The lesson we describe on the following pages relates to the chapter book *My Name Is Mar'a Isabel* by Alma Flor Ada (Atheneum, 1993), a book Maria has selected for a unit exploring immigration, something many of her students or their parents have experienced first hand. Maria has used Book Club *Plus* (Raphael, Florio-Ruane, George, Hasty, & Highfield, 2004) to organize her literacy instruction, as shown in Figure 3.2.

The three-phase lesson described here occurs within the Book Club component. First, there is a whole-class opening share, during which Maria introduces the chapter book and sets the text in the context of the study of immigration. Second, students read the relevant chapters (in her classroom, some students are reading the English version of the book and others the Spanish version) and write their responses to an In the Book QAR in their reading logs. Third, students gather on the carpet for a whole-class discussion during a closing community share. The flow of the QARs used in each phase reflects the cycle depicted in Figure 3.2.

Before Reading

Before reading, three theme questions are posted to guide discussion that morning:

* Why do people move?
* What are the lives of immigrants in America like?
* How can we learn from other people's experiences?

Figure 3.2 *Book Club* **Plus** *Literacy Framework*

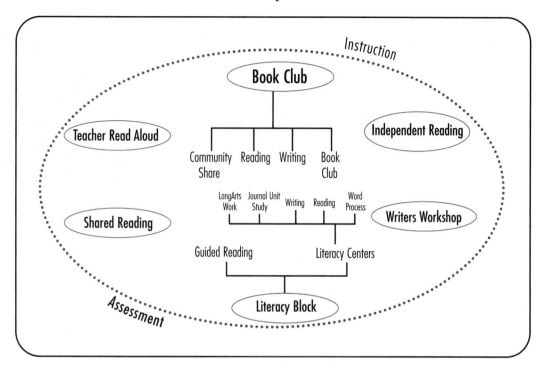

Notice that all questions are from the In My Head QAR category, specifically On My Own—questions of the type readers would expect to have prior to reading a book. The three questions are written on a sheet of large chart paper near where the students have gathered on the carpet, so they can refer to them easily. The students face Maria, who is seated in a rocking chair. Maria starts the discussion by reading the first question and reminding her students of earlier readings and conversations that they will want to draw upon to answer the question.

Maria: The first question, "Why do people move?" We've read three or four books already, and there are different reasons why people move. Why did people move from the South to the North. Okay, wait, I'm going to give you fifteen seconds to think about it and then I want hands up. Okay? Ready? *(She then repeats the directions quietly in Spanish as students think.)*

Maria gives students plenty of time—15 seconds is long in most whole-class lessons. As she waits, several students' hands pop up. This wait time is valuable for all students, but especially for those who do not speak English as their first language. Maria calls on Esteban, who says, "They moved because they needed a better life, because they didn't have money." While this is accurate, Maria has been teaching students about extended responses in answer to In My Head and Think & Search QARs, so in the following exchange, we can see how she, just as Ms. Jones did in Chapter 2, elicits more information from Esteban. As she calls on other students, she explicitly notes they are building on one another's ideas as they answer the questions.

Maria: Okay, "better life," that's good. What do you mean by "better life"? That's a general term, right? Okay. *(She signals Esteban to continue with a nod.)*

Esteban: For a better job.

Maria: Okay, for a better job. What was another reason? *(She nods at Tyrone, who has his hand in the air.)* Go ahead.

As Tyrone answers, Sam chimes in and the teacher nods "okay" to both of them. Tyrone takes up Sam's comment and incorporates it into his own. (Note that when speakers are simultaneously speaking, the overlapping words are underlined.)

Tyrone: The war had doubled the cost of food—

Sam: For the poor

Maria: Okay. *(Nods okay.)*

Tyrone: and made life harder for the poor.

Maria again prompts them to extend their answer by asking another In My Head question and reminding them of the strategy—recalling or remembering what they have read and discussed in the earlier texts. "What war? Remember?" she asks. Several students respond together, saying, "the first one," "World War I," and "the First World War." While the actual terms of QAR do not explicitly come up in this particular exchange, Maria is using the public and social space of her classroom—Quadrant I, as we described in Chapter 2—to create an important opportunity to make explicit the kinds of QARs one encounters before reading. Such questions require students to go to their heads, use their memories, and think about other books they have read. They use this information as they consider the range of reasons why people like the family in the book decide to immigrate to a new country. Maria then asks the students to think about a book they read earlier in this unit, *Hannah's Journal*, by Marissa Moss (Turtleback Books, 2002). She reminds them that they have learned about the importance of work to new immigrants. As you read the dialogue, notice how she reinforces the importance of remembering earlier readings and building on one another's ideas.

Maria: Remember the book *Hannah's Journal*? *(Several students can be heard murmuring uh-huhs and yeahs/yeses.)* How was her life in America?

Sonia: She went to school.

Maria: She went to school, but what else?

Several students: Jobs!

Maria: *(smiling)* She had to go to work.

Esteban: And she also had to get tickets for her mom and dad. Then they could come to America.

Maria: So you're building on her comment. She worked so <u>she could get the money</u>—

Esteban: <u>She could buy the ticket</u>, the twenty-five dollars!

Maria uses the discussion to model for students the importance of thinking about what you know. She reminds them that one source of what they know comes from remembering information from earlier encounters with texts, and she emphasizes the importance of building on one another's ideas to extend their responses to the In My Head questions they were discussing.

During Reading

During their reading, Maria emphasizes ways students can make sense of what they are reading. She reminds them to use previously learned strategies such as

* making connections between how the characters are feeling and how they would feel in the same situation;

* using predictions both to monitor their understanding and to make inferences about the connection between current and future story events; and

* drawing on their knowledge of story elements to develop a clear concept of what is happening over time and how characters grow and change.

Following the opening community-share discussion, students read the first chapter of the book either in English or in Spanish, and they are all expected to use their reading logs to record their thinking. This is a typical way for teachers to trace students' thinking in the private contexts that characterize Quadrants II and III of the Vygotsky Space. For this part of the lesson, students are seated at their desks with their books and reading logs. As Maria gets them started on independent reading, she gives them an overarching Think & Search question to guide their thinking about the important information in this first chapter, "How does Mar'a feel about her first day of school?" She then reminds them about what they have learned from QAR to make their log entries more valuable.

> **Maria:** Before you start, I'm going to make one gesture and you're going to know what I mean, right? *(She holds one hand to each side and moves as if she were walking on a balance beam.)* What are the most important things that you do?
>
> **Several students, at once:** Balancing our ideas with the author, with a text.

The idea of balancing information sources and using both the ideas in the text and the ideas in their head is a central point to teaching students about QAR. Once they understand this concept, a gesture such as the one Maria uses prompts them. Maria then reminds them of the importance of using information from the text to support their answers, and tells them explicitly that they must "find evidence from the text" to support their log entries.

As students read and write in their logs, Maria roams the room, stopping for mini-conferences with individual students. These conferences reinforce students' effective use of the information sources—text and head—that underlie QAR. Several students' log entries begin with the phrase "In the book it said" or "In the text." Stopping by Mariana's desk, Maria stoops so she is at the same level as Mariana's book and log. Maria asks Mariana to tell her about her log entry, which indicates that she thinks Mar'a Isabel feels *mal* (bad). The conversation was conducted in Spanish:

Maria: Bad, why?

Mariana: Because she doesn't know anyone.

Maria: It says so in the book, right? Show me that part in the book.

Notice the repetition of the QAR language "in the book" as part of the fabric of the ongoing conversation. Mariana begins to turn through the pages of the first chapter to find the information she used to answer the question and then reads the segment aloud to Maria. Pushing on the idea of balance, Maria invites her to think about her own knowledge, "So, there's the idea in the book. What's your idea about that?" Mariana responds by pointing to another section of her log in which she has written, "Perhaps the other children will make fun of her." Maria agrees that this is something that children would worry about, again reinforcing the importance of, and Mariana's success in, balancing ideas in the text with ideas in her head as she reads and constructs meaning.

After Reading

After reading, during the closing community share, Maria has the opportunity to teach and reinforce questions from the Author & Me QAR category. Students have concluded that Mar'a Isabel is going to feel scared and nervous on her first day of school. Maria uses this conclusion to show that Author & Me QARs lead to reading between the lines—that the text never explicitly says that this is how Mar'a Isabel will feel. Instead there is "evidence in the text" that the students used to help them figure out their conclusion—which came from their heads. She leads a discussion in which students build on a number of telling details they found in the text: Mar'a couldn't eat; her book bag felt very heavy even though there weren't many books in it; she was not wanting to go to school; and so forth. Students know that Author & Me QARs require them to use information from their heads, but the information they use must make sense in light of the evidence in the text.

This pattern of strategy use before, during, and after reading is relatively consistent, though there is no one single pathway through a text. Figure 3.3 provides an example of a chart used in a middle school classroom to help students understand the alignment between the QARs and the kinds of questions asked before, during, and after reading. On this chart, the teacher and her students have identified generic questions within each QAR category that can guide reading throughout the cycle.

When students have a firm understanding of the language of QAR, teachers are better able to teach explicitly, model, and scaffold appropriate ways of engaging with the text across the entire reading cycle: before, during, and after reading.

Comprehension Strategies and QAR

Capable readers understand that comprehension is a complex process made up of many individual strategies (predicting, summarizing, making inferences, and so on). Successful readers may simultaneously visualize and make an inference. They understand that there is no one right strategy or combination of strategies that should be used to make sense of texts. Thus, comprehension instruction requires that you teach components of an overall process and do so in a way that ensures that students are mastering individual strategies. Students may lose sight of the purpose of comprehension strategies when they are taught them out of context and then practice them in isolation on worksheets. For example, high-quality comprehension instruction that focuses on visualizing text would have students write the images that come to mind when reading real texts that have rich, descriptive language rather than isolated sentences on a work sheet.

We have found that using QAR as a framework for organizing comprehension instruction helps achieve two important goals.

Figure 3.3 *QAR and the Reading Cycle in a Middle School Classroom*

	QARs and Sample Questions
Before Reading	**On My Own** • From the title or the topic, what do I already know that can connect me to the story/text? **Author & Me** • From the topic, title, illustrations, and/or book cover, what might this story/text be about?
During Reading	**Author & Me** • What do I think will happen next? How would I describe the mood of the story and why is this important? **Think and Search** • What is the problem and how is it resolved? • What role do [*insert characters' names*] play in the story? • What are the important events? (literary, informational) **Right There** • Who is the main character? (literary) • Identify the topic sentence in this paragraph. (informational) • What are some words that describe the setting? (literary)
After Reading	**Author & Me** • What is the author's message? • What is the theme and how is it connected to the world beyond the story? • How can I synthesize the information with what I know from other sources? • How well does the author make his/her argument? • How is the author using particular language to influence my beliefs? **Think and Search** • Find evidence in the text to support an argument.

(1) Students learn to align the different QARs with the before-during-after reading cycle. (2) Students learn to align the different QARs with particular comprehension strategies. The alignment of QAR with comprehension strategies and the reading cycle happens simultaneously. Students learn which comprehension strategies are the most effective for particular QARs within specific components of the reading cycle: Prior to reading, they are more likely to encounter On My Own QARs, and strategies for answering such QARs include accessing background knowledge and visualizing. In contrast, during reading they are more likely to encounter Right There QARs, which call for strategies such as skimming or scanning. Using QAR as a framework gives students more control over strategy use and strategic thinking during reading.

Identify Core Comprehension Strategies

Making sure that students get a handle on core categories or clusters of strategies that can be used consistently within and across grade levels is central to effective comprehension-strategy instruction. For struggling readers especially, it is helpful to have consistent language and categories. Many useful resources are available that review the research on comprehension and comprehension instruction (see, for example, Dole, Duffy, Roehler, & Pearson, 1991; Pearson & Fielding, 1991; Pressley, 2002; Raphael & Brock, 1997). Though strategies have been described in many different ways, these reviews of this large body of research suggest they can be grouped into six categories: predicting, identifying important information, summarizing, making inferences, questioning, and monitoring.

Each of these categories encompasses a range of strategies that can be taught, and teachers can use QAR to plan what to teach, when to teach it, and how to describe its purpose within the bigger picture of making sense of text.

For example, as illustrated in Figure 3.4, making inferences can include strategies such as imagining how a character might feel, visualizing, and reading between the lines. Summarizing strategies can include using graphic organizers to display key ideas, selecting key information and deleting unnecessary material, and using story structure to highlight key points in a narrative. Questioning strategies can include generating questions for inquiry projects or book clubs (student-led discussions), as well as distinguishing among types of questions.

Combining Strategies

Good readers tend to use a combination of strategies as they read. Imagine yourself sitting in a comfortable chair. In your hand is a book that a close friend, a neighbor, or a colleague has recommended. You enter the world of this text, activating relevant background knowledge to help you construct meaning as you read. You fill in implicit information by making inferences, perhaps a self-to-text connection. You predict what might happen, and when your predictions do not pan out, you monitor to see if the author meant to surprise you (and thus your comprehension hasn't been compromised) or if you have missed something (and perhaps need to reread an earlier section).

You determine what is important as you go, holding that information in mind while letting lesser details go. You may question the text, wondering why you are being led in a particular direction, questioning a character's motives, or in an informational text, perhaps asking yourself questions to monitor your degree of understanding. Good readers do not use a single strategy; they have mastered individual strategies and use them together effectively. These capable readers understand how strategies work together and are applied effectively before, during, and after reading.

We believe that to create highly capable readers, teachers need to teach both the individual strategies and the way these individual strategies work together. Such instruction requires time for students to be introduced to the concepts (Quadrant I of the Vygotsky Space) and opportunities for them to practice and apply what they have been taught (Quadrants II and III). Students need to encounter increasingly sophisticated comprehension strategies and to see how they connect across the six categories and how they build on earlier strategies. It is not as important what labels teachers use for these strategies as it is

Figure 3.4 *Six Categories of Comprehension Strategies*

Comprehension Category	Selected Sample Strategies

Predicting: *Creating a hypothesis based on back-ground knowledge, text features, and text structure about upcoming information in a text.*	• Hypothesizing about what the author might discuss next in the text
	• Using relevant sources of information for predicting, such as
	  • Background knowledge the reader already possesses
	  • Text features such as titles, headings, and embedded questions
	  • Text structures—how the text is organized
	• Setting a purpose for reading: Confirming content or disproving hypotheses (connects to monitoring if prediction is not confirmed—does it indicate comprehension block or is the author successfully "surprising" the reader?)
	• Engaging in appropriate routines such as taking a picture-walk or a book-walk or using knowledge of parts of the text—index, title, TOC, illustrations—to predict

Identifying Important Information: *Identifying the superordinate, driving idea in a section of text; distinguishing this superordinate idea from the details that elaborate on it.*	• Recognizing that some ideas are more important than others in a passage • Distinguishing between main ideas and supporting details • Identifying key story elements • Underlining or highlighting the sentence or phrase that captures the important information presented in a paragraph • Understanding the gist or overall topic • Identifying key words or phrases • Making use of text structure to identify key ideas • Distinguishing between author-determined versus reader-determined importance
Summarizing: *Creating a new, succinct text that encompasses the important information in the section of text being summarized.*	• Making use of story structure to highlight key points in a narrative • Composing a brief, new text based on important ideas already identified • Synthesizing text ideas in a succinct and coherent fashion • Integrating material into a coherent, accurate representation (such as a graphic organizer) • Distinguishing between writer-based and reader-based summaries • Selecting key information and deleting unnecessary or redundant material • Condensing some material • Substituting superordinate concepts (e.g., wild animals for lions, tigers, bears) • Composing a topic sentence • Composing a thesis statement • Distinguishing between summarizing and retelling

Making Inferences: *Reading "between the lines" to add information not explicitly stated by the author but needed to make sense of the text.*	• Reading more than the words, or "between the lines" • Accessing prior knowledge triggered by information or words provided by the author • Seeing connections among text ideas, when those connections have not been explicitly stated by the author • Making text-to-self, text-to-text, and text-to-world connections • Visualizing or creating mental images based on the text • Thinking of contexts in which the information learned might be useful • Imagining how a character might feel • Identifying with a character • Interpreting the author's message • Creating a theme or thesis for the text • Distinguishing between literal and figurative meanings
Questioning: *Using knowledge for answering and asking questions, including creating relevant questions to guide reading for explicit and implicit text information, drawing on both the reader's knowledge base and information presented by the text.*	• Setting purposes or goals for reading • Clarifying confusions or confusing information • Determining the author's position or intention in writing the piece (this begins to get at critical thinking and evaluation) • Distinguishing among types of questions and knowing when to ask what kind (e.g., eliciting factual and explicit information; inferences that can be made with text information; critical and evaluative text interpretation; author's craft and style; relationships among texts) • Understanding sources of information for creating questions and, thus, better understanding where appropriate information is found for answering questions
Monitoring: *Evaluating text understanding and using fix-up strategies appropriately in the face of comprehension difficulties.*	• Evaluating understanding and appropriateness of the strategies used to learn from text • Establishing goals and consciously evaluating the degree to which the goals are being met • Modifying strategies when necessary to read goals (i.e., having a repertoire of strategies to draw on in appropriate circumstances • Determining whether or not the text read makes sense based on expectations (can get at this by paraphrasing, checking predictions against current understanding of text information, clarifying) • Knowing reasons why text might not have made sense (e.g., unfamiliar vocabulary, awkward structure, unclear referent words, idiomatic expressions) • Key strategies for teaching monitoring include question-asking before, during, and after reading; working collaboratively to answer questions because students must clarify their understandings when explaining to another student

that they use the chosen labels consistently. Doing so will show students how what they are learning builds across grade levels as well as across contexts within grade levels, an idea we discuss extensively in Chapter 6. As a result of careful planning and instruction, students should be able both to appropriate what they have learned and to transform it to meet the ever increasing demands they will face from a range of texts.

Aligning Strategies With QAR

We've shown you how QAR aligns with the reading cycle and how individual comprehension strategies can be grouped into six manageable categories. Figure 3.5 shows how QAR aligns with many comprehension strategies. At each grade level, you should be teaching the comprehension strategies that align with the QARs that students are addressing. In this way, readers will understand what expectations are required of them before, during, or after reading. They will learn the appropriate strategies for generating successful responses and creating effective questions. Let's take a closer look at how each QAR relates to comprehension instruction.

Comprehension Instruction and Right There QARs

 The purpose of students creating or responding to Right There questions is to make them aware of the important details that support key ideas in the text. Simply finding the details is often a challenge for them. Unfortunately, too many students choose rereading as their sole strategy for answering Right There questions, when in fact they also need to learn to use scanning effectively, develop note-taking strategies, and learn to draw on specific context clues. Comprehension instruction for Right There QARs focuses on

❋ teaching students *multiple* strategies for answering Right There questions,

Figure 3.5 *Using QAR to Frame Comprehension Strategy Instruction*

QAR	Sample Comprehension Strategies
Right There	1. Scanning to locate information 2. Note-taking strategies to support easier recall of key information 3. Using context clues for creating definitions
Think & Search	1. Identifying important information 2. Summarizing 3. Using text organization (e.g., comparison-contrast, problem-solution, list, explanation) to identify relevant information 4. Visualizing (e.g., setting, mood, procedures) 5. Using context to describe symbols and figurative language 6. Clarifying 7. Making text-to-text connections 8. Making simple inferences
Author & Me	1. Predicting 2. Visualizing 3. Making simple and complex inferences 4. Distinguishing fact and opinion 5. Making text-to-self connections
On My Own	1. Activating prior knowledge (about genre, experiences, authors, etc.) 2. Connecting to the topic (self-to-text)

❋ establishing a clear purpose for the strategies, and

❋ articulating when they might encounter Right There questions that call upon these strategies.

Students learn the strategy, when and how it might be applied, and why it is useful. They begin to build an understanding of the control they have as readers as they work to make sense of text.

Comprehension Instruction and Think & Search QARs

 Delivering an extended oral or written response to a question often involves pulling together information from multiple places in the text, which can be difficult for students. In the original QAR research, Taffy Raphael and David Pearson (1985) found that the Think & Search category was one of the most challenging areas of questioning activities within comprehension. To successfully handle a Think & Search QAR, readers must be able to identify important information, understand how text is organized, and synthesize the information in a meaningful way. Today, we see students experiencing similar challenges on the extended-response items on state tests (e.g., the Illinois State Achievement Test, or ISAT).

There are many strategies that can help students with the task demands of Think & Search QARs, such as creating or using graphic organizers so they can map the information in terms of relevance and hierarchical importance; using visualization strategies so that they can see the sequence of tasks or events relevant to meaning making (e.g., in planning to conduct a science experiment or in understanding relevant aspects of the setting of a story); and using summarizing strategies, of which there are many research-based choices.

Kathy Highfield, in working with her fourth-grade students, makes several instructional decisions related to what to teach within this category. For example, she knows that over the course of the school year she will teach students to reread strategically and look for key words that will signal the most important information. She will show how key words may vary across a science, social studies, or literary text segment. She will use many lifted texts (Harvey & Goudvis, 2000) to illustrate these key words. Science and social studies texts often use bold or italicized fonts or headings to convey an important idea. Images in these texts also may communicate key ideas. In stories, however, key ideas depend on the genre and particular story elements. When students have a sense of how the text information can guide their rereading, they are in a better position to draw on strategies for thinking about the main idea, summarizing, and understanding the difference between retelling and summarizing.

Comprehension Instruction and Author & Me QARs

 Author & Me QARs provide an excellent, practical context for helping students understand the importance of comprehension strategies that help them link text information to their own experience. Critical reading requires students to be able to distinguish fact from opinion, make both simple and complex inferences from the information that has been presented, make judgments about how they would respond in situations faced by characters in the stories they read, visualize settings and events from text information that presents only a partial picture, and make predictions about what may happen next—whether it's in the context of fiction, history, or a science experiment. Capable readers are expected to make text-to-self connections as well as text-to-theme and text-to-world connections. Critical readers have to be able to integrate what they read with what they know.

You can ground comprehension-strategy instruction as well as instruction in response to literature in students' understanding of Author & Me QARs. Doing so provides students with a way to organize the many different approaches, which can often seem like unrelated tasks. QAR provides you and your students with a language to make connections among the different strategies they are learning and the purposes that they can serve. For example, with Author & Me QARs, students learn to make text-to-self connections that explicitly make visible the need to balance personal experience with what they are reading in the texts. They learn to make inferences, which involves reading between the lines of the text and using their own experience to determine information that is not stated. With a shared QAR vocabulary, students will see that both strategies share a common foundation—the ability to link ideas from the text to what they already know.

Comprehension Instruction and On My Own QARs

You know how important it is for students to think about what they already know before they read. Activating prior knowledge is a key comprehension strategy that can be taught in many ways. Donna Ogle's K-W-L approach is a classic way to get students to think about what they already know about a topic, set their own goals for reading, and evaluate what they have learned (Ogle, 1986). Starting a unit with On My Own questions is another way. Maria Ruiz Blanco asks On My Own questions at the start of every unit she teaches. As they answer the questions, students identify relevant background knowledge and share their knowledge with one another.

Using QAR to Frame Comprehension Instruction: Creating a Plan

Kathy Highfield uses QAR in her fourth-grade class to frame comprehension instruction. Her goal is to move students away from learning isolated reading comprehension strategies in guided reading groups to learning them embedded in QAR instruction. First, Kathy explicitly explains to her students that they will be focusing on learning the reading comprehension strategies that they will be using throughout the reading cycle. She explains that thinking about questions related to each phase of the reading cycle will help them better understand when to use specific comprehension strategies. Next, Kathy uses a Think Aloud to model the type of thinking she expects students to do. She reads a section of text and models how capable readers ask questions before, during, and after reading. As she applies specific reading comprehension strategies (skimming, remembering from first reading, rereading, looking for key words, etc.) she writes each on a sticky note, explains the strategy aloud, and puts the note on a chart (similar to the one shown in Figure 3.5). Next, she gives students the full text and has them work in pairs. She tells them to practice thinking aloud as they work and list all of their reading strategies on a class poster. Kathy walks around the room and assists students who need additional scaffolding. When students are done, they come back together as a class and discuss the strategies they have listed. The class decides which strategies they would be more likely to use during each phase of the reading cycle. The poster they have created remains on the wall throughout the entire year. At times, strategies are added, removed, or moved around to fit students' growing and changing knowledge about QAR.

In its role as a common classroom language that enables students to understand how comprehension strategies help them ask and answer questions successfully, to comprehend a wide range of texts, QAR has become part of the fabric of Kathy's classroom communication across subject areas and grade levels.

The Power of QAR in Peer-Led Discussions

Tyisha is a fifth grader at Boone Elementary School in Chicago. She and her class have been working with QAR. Tyisha sits at her desk preparing for her upcoming book club discussion with four of her peers. They have read the chapter called "Peaches" in the book *Esperanza Rising* by Pam Muñoz Ryan (Scholastic, 2000) and are writing comments, questions, personal connections, and other entries in their reading logs so that when they meet for their student-led discussions they are each prepared to make substantive contributions. Today, Tyisha has decided to generate a series of questions—primarily Author & Me questions and a few On My Owns—that she believes will lead to a deep discussion about important ideas in the story.

In this section of the book, issues of discrimination are prominent. One character, a third grader named Isabel, hopes to become Queen of the May, despite the fact, as Esperanza knows, that teachers never select students of color or those whose native language is not English. Miguel, Esperanza's friend and her late father's protégé, hopes to become an engineer but has just been pulled off such work and told to dig ditches. Esperanza finds out that a new pool is being put into the migrant work camps where the Oklahomans will be housed. Mexican children will be

(continued on following page)

(continued from preceding page)

able to use the pool only on Friday, before it is to be cleaned. Tyisha's questions prompt her peers to consider how they would feel and what they would do and to make interpretations:

* How would you feel if you saw Isabel sitting there saying that she wanted to be Queen of the May?

* Would you tell Isabel that the teachers pick only the blonde and blue-eyed girls?

* How would you feel if you are Mexican and you only could swim on Friday before they clean the pool?

* How do you think Miguel felt when Esperanza asked, "Why did you dig ditches?" Would you feel the same way as Miguel?

* What do you think the meteor [sic: metaphor] "Wait a while, the fruit will fall in your hand" meant?

To understand most of these questions and answer them in meaningful ways, students would have to read about Isabel, identify things that she was trying to do to become Queen of the May (e.g., achieve good grades, have perfect attendance), and understand the teachers' biases (i.e., that preferring people with blue eyes reflected a set of prejudices against the immigrants in the community). They would need to unpack the behavior of Miguel's boss and the owners of the migrant camps to see the connections between their behavior and that of Isabel's teachers. But to address the questions successfully, they also have to draw on their own experiences and beliefs.

For example, in response to the second question, students debated whether or not Esperanza should tell Isabel. Some argued it was only fair to tell her, so Isabel would not be disappointed, while others argued that this is a situation that Isabel cannot change, so why tell her and cause her to lose hope? Still others suggested that Esperanza couldn't know for sure what would happen, that there might be a substitute teacher that day and Isabel may have a chance. One student pointed out that *esperanza* means hope in Spanish and that this might mean that they should always have hope. They used comprehension strategies that included identifying important information, using supporting details, asking questions, and making inferences. They knew how to apply these strategies appropriately as they read and talked about the book. They were able to support their claims using evidence from the text. They could scan the text for relevant details. And they were using multiple strategies in combination to engage in discussion at high levels of literacy.

Since the goals of good comprehension instruction are to ensure that students are able to establish clear purposes for their reading, apply background knowledge, and make inferences and intertextual and text-to-person connections, we can recognize these students as being very successful. The students use their knowledge of QAR in the practice of making meaning from text. They know the strategies that help answer each type of QAR and they can apply what they know to both asking and answering questions.

Concluding Comments

We hope QAR instruction will help students develop and own the metacognitive knowledge necessary to be successful readers and provide them with the language for using this knowledge effectively—what Scott Paris and his colleagues call the "skill" and "will" characteristics of successful readers. We want students to be readers who can describe what a strategy is, how it works, and when and why to use it (Paris, Lipson & Wixson, 1983). Kathy Highfield's fourth graders have exactly this type of attitude and knowledge. When students understand QAR and how it can be used in different settings, researchers have found that they continue to use it for at least eight months (Ezell, Hunsicker, & Quinque, 1997). Kathy has observed similar lasting effects. At the end of the school year, she asked her students to think about QAR in their own lives—within and outside their language arts time, as well as in and out of school.

During the free-flowing discussion, students brainstormed a broad array of applications, showing that they not only had appropriated QAR for use in conventional reading activities but had transformed what they had learned. Jefferson, for example, shared that he had used QAR in math class while he was working on a story problem. He described how he read the problem and then listed what he already knew about multiplication that would help him solve it. Then he used information from the story problem to figure out what needed to be multiplied. He thought that this was a good example of how Author & Me helped remind him that he shouldn't just pick any two numbers from a problem to multiply, but rather that he had to figure out which were the right numbers to use.

Alex drew on an activity as far from the classroom as one could imagine. She had a horse on her family's small farm. She vividly described how that week she had used strategies from QAR to search for the horse's bridle. She said that when she went into the barn to get her horse ready, she noticed that the bridle was not "right there" on the peg where it should have been. She said she had to "think and search" for it until she found it—using all the evidence in the barn to help her figure out where it might be. But she also had to remember (in her head) what she had done when she was there last. She ended by saying that she knew she would find the bridle by thinking and searching, and knowing this helped her not give up!

Edie summarized how she thought about QAR quite simply. She said, "I will use it on everything. It's just part of who I am" (Highfield, 2003). That is the goal for QAR instruction—making it part of the repertoire of deep-thinking skills that students can use in a variety of contexts. In Chapter 4 we turn to an examination of how QAR instruction varies across grade levels and subject areas.

Chapter 4

Teaching QAR Across Grades and Content Areas

*M*r. Jefferson's eighth graders are working through how scientists think about their research. Their teacher is explaining the concept of a hypothesis that a scientist or a team of scientists creates to drive their inquiry. But his students are struggling with the idea that scientists' hypotheses are grounded in their own research or that of other scientists. They do not understand that new inquiry questions arise from what the scientists already know. To his students, research is a mysterious process and the idea of where research questions come from is, for the moment, out of their reach. In contrast, Hannah Natividad's sixth graders have some insight into where research questions come from. They describe a hypothesis as being like an Author & Me, sort of like a prediction. Scientists think about what they know (the "me" in Author & Me) and about what others have written about what they want to study (the "author"). When they put it together, they make a guess about what they think will happen in their experiments. The difference between these two groups of students is not necessarily one of ability, but one of language. In Hannah's classroom, she and her students have a language to talk about complex constructs that describe how knowledge develops and the relationship among what we can learn from text, what we already know, and what we can predict from combining this information to form a hypothesis. Hannah's students see the parallel between testing a prediction during reading and testing a hypothesis through scientific procedures. The value of QAR, once the core concepts have been introduced in a classroom, lies in its power to facilitate classroom talk across not only grade levels but also content areas. QAR underscores the ways in which what we have learned in one context provides support for learning in new settings.

Because of variations in students' ages and the scope of their knowledge of QAR, you need to be creative about how you introduce and extend students' knowledge of QAR. In this chapter, we build on the foundations that have been laid in the first three chapters, which introduced the key concepts underlying QAR instruction for all students (Chapter 1), explained the instructional model for initial QAR instruction in any classroom or subject area (Chapter 2), and detailed how QAR provides a framework for comprehension instruction (Chapter 3). We'll begin by considering the implications that variations in students' QAR knowledge have for instructional decisions and curriculum planning. Then we'll describe the instructional practices of teachers from a variety of grade levels and subject areas who have been successful in teaching their students about QAR and show how to apply these practices in a range of settings.

Planning for Teaching QAR

When creating QAR instructional plans, we suggest that you think about five basic factors:

1. **What your students already know about QAR**

2. **End-of-year goals for students**

3. **Time in the school year when QAR is being introduced and used**

4. **Ways to incorporate QAR language and thinking throughout the day and across curriculum areas**

5. **Student motivation and engagement**

We'll look at each of these factors in depth.

1. You should consider **what your students already know about QAR**, which may vary for many reasons. For example, Shields Elementary School in Chicago decided to use QAR in all grade levels to frame its whole-school goal of improving comprehension instruction (see Chapter 6). In the fall of the first year of this effort, no students had any knowledge of QAR. Regardless of grade level, teachers introduced their students to the two primary information sources (In the Book, In My Head) and then, as appropriate for the grade level, continued with the introduction of the four core categories. In the second year of the effort, with the exception of first grade, teachers were working with students who had learned about and used the language of QAR the previous year. Teachers had to review, and then could quickly build upon, what students had done previously. By the third year, all students (except first graders and transfer students) had still more experience using QAR, and so on throughout the years and grade levels. Instructional plans must take into account students' background in QAR and provide for differentiated instruction to address these variations.

2. In planning QAR instruction, set **end-of-year goals** that take into account the QAR knowledge that students will be expected to have at the next grade level. For example, fourth- and fifth-grade teachers in one school knew that by middle school their students would need a firm command of how to use graphic

organizers to answer a range of Think & Search QARs that depended on readers' knowledge of how text is structured. The fourth-grade teachers agreed to introduce their students to applications with graphic organizers and texts that included organizational structures, such as lists, explanations, sequences, and compare-and-contrasts and to give their students ample opportunity to practice with them. Fifth-grade teachers agreed to review those organizational structures and add the problem-and-solution and cause-and-effect structures.

3. Make decisions about **when in the school year QAR will be introduced**. For example, Taffy Raphael and Kathryn Au (2001) recommend introducing the QAR categories to be used in a particular grade level early in the school year. This will maximize the time that students will have to internalize and transform them for use in a variety of contexts—as was demonstrated by Kathy Highfield's students at the end of Chapter 3. However, we also recommend conducting "booster lessons," during which the QAR knowledge introduced early in the year is systematically taught, with the six-step instructional model, in new areas. For example, you may put together a six-step lesson (see Chapter 2) to show students how to use QAR with a math story problem, a science selection, or a sample test passage (see Chapter 5 for more on QAR and test-taking skills). In this way, at every grade level students learn that QAR is applicable beyond the reading or language arts classroom.

4. Plan **ways to use QAR systematically as part of day-to-day classroom studies** and communication. As we demonstrate through examples later in the chapter, you can use QAR language in social studies, science, or math, to prepare for book club or literature discussions, to create good inquiry questions, to identify information needed to solve problems, or to take the mystery out of classroom and high-stakes tests. If instructional planning includes opportunities for students to extend their use of QAR in new and innovative ways, students are more likely to transform what they have learned about QAR. Otherwise they may just use strategies in the contexts in which they learned them.

5. Plan instruction that will continue to **motivate students** to learn about QAR as they go deeper into categories and related comprehension strategies. The concepts underlying QAR are so straightforward that it makes it easy for teachers to apply what they know about good teaching to maintain students' interest and engagement. For example, we'll see later in the chapter how a middle school teacher created a *Jeopardy!* type of game in which her students compete in teams. The game provided important practice in generating questions and identifying QARs, yet avoided

Figure 4.1 *Ways to Motivate Students*

Let students see teacher and peer modeling of strategy use.
- Use teacher modeling so students see exactly what they have to do and aren't afraid to try.
- Use peer modeling to allow students to see how other students are applying the strategy, which may be in a more realistic and less proficient manner than the teacher.

Use interesting texts.
- Base strategy lessons on high-interest texts.
- On occasion, let a group of students choose a text they think others would find interesting, and develop a strategy lesson around this text.

Show students the usefulness of the strategies.
- Have students share how the strategies have helped them with ongoing classroom activities and tasks.
- Make connections between the strategies and the materials students read outside of school, such as magazines and Web pages.

Provide social support for strategy use.
- Have students work in small groups, situations that give students access to peer modeling and help.
- Give help to struggling readers as needed, and pair these students with others.

Have students engage in goal setting and self-assessment.
- Have students develop goals for strategy application, making sure that the goals are attainable and short-term.
- On a regular basis, give students the chance to engage in self-assessment, to measure progress toward meeting their goals, receive additional help if necessary, and celebrate advancement.

Sources: Schunk & Zimmerman, 1997. Guthrie & Wigfield, 2000.

the tedium of a workbook. This instructional principle underscores the importance of affect and attitude—students can become bored even with very useful strategies if they do not have opportunities to engage with them in creative ways. A summary of some of the research on how to motivate students is included in Figure 4.1.

Based on these factors, a central tenet for planning appropriate QAR instruction is

> Introduce students to the core QARs for the grade level within the first few weeks of school and then extend QAR language to the day-to-day operations of the classroom.

In the first few weeks of school, we suggest that you introduce or conduct initial reviews of QAR, working through the paired comparisons appropriate to the students. For example, introduce only In the Book and In My Head to first graders. In third grade, begin with them and elaborate on them until students have control over the four core QARs: Right There, Think & Search, Author & Me, and On My Own.

After this initial instruction, be sure you reinforce students' knowledge of QAR language through day-to-day use of the terms in the context of reading, writing, and talking about text. When students are confident in their QAR knowledge, extend it by applying it to the texts and genres important to the grade level, and to the classroom interactions—such as book club discussions, guided reading groups, inquiry activities, math story problems, and other school subject areas—relevant to their work across the school year.

Planning Relevant Instruction Within and Across Grade Levels

Teachers we've worked with who consider the factors described above for planning QAR instruction have found many opportunities to extend the introductory lessons using the six-step instructional model. The primary, intermediate, and middle school classrooms presented below capture differences in the ways QAR is taught across grade levels and school subjects.

Primary Grades: Reading and Book Club Discussions

When Jennifer McClorey, the first-grade teacher mentioned in Chapter 1 who had developed the QAR flip cards (Figure 1.8), introduces QAR to her students, it is the first time many of the children have heard about it. She is responsible for teaching them the initial concepts and explaining how QAR can help them throughout the school day. She begins by teaching students to distinguish In the Book and In My Head QARs. Most of her students are emergent readers, so shared reading time is a critical setting for teaching the initial concepts. By reading aloud as students follow along, she gives them a chance to concentrate on thinking about QAR knowledge sources, rather than on decoding. Jennifer also supports her students by writing questions on sentence strips and reading them to the students, rather than asking students to write questions during small-group and whole-class lessons. To practice generating questions, students say them as Jennifer writes them on sentence strips. By taking responsibility for writing, Jennifer is allowing students to concentrate on developing their questions.

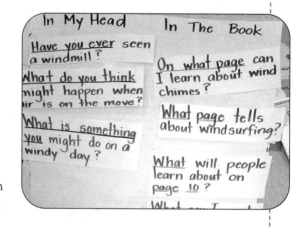

Jennifer uses visual and hands-on means to keep students involved. The flip cards she developed have illustrations for the key words *head* and *book* so students can concentrate on the QAR instead of the text on the cards. Jen asks students who have chosen different QARs to explain their selections. This reminds students that they must be able to justify their answers. When teaching about In the Book QARs, Jennifer has students come up to the shared-reading Big Book and point to where they looked for the answer. She models and then asks them to slide their finger across the words as she reads them. She asks them to put sticky notes next to illustrations that provide information. Students point to their heads when they use information from their background knowledge or place a sticky note with a picture of a head on the page in the book to which they made the connection. Jennifer's instructional planning focuses on

* the **content** of what she will teach about QAR—that there are two main sources of information, In the Book and In My Head;

* the **strategies** associated with each QAR (e.g., using pictures and text for information or taking a picture walk for In the Book; making a self-to-text connection or thinking about our personal experiences for In My Head); and

* **how she will engage** her students in thinking about QAR (e.g., through manipulatives, Big Books during shared reading, sentence strips).

Janine Rodrigues is another first-grade teacher who was introduced in Chapter 1. Like Maria Ruiz Blanco, whom we met in Chapter 3, Janine has worked with her students to teach them the vocabulary of QAR specifically to enhance book club log entries and discussions (Raphael et al., 2004). For book club, her students read a section of a book—often one of a series of picture books related to a common theme, such as Being a Good Friend or Grandparents in Our Lives. They write key questions worthy of discussion on sticky-notes. They respond to one another's questions in pairs, then in small student-led

QAR Now: Question Answer Relationships

discussion groups (four to six students). In their reading logs, they answer questions Janine has created to push their thinking further.

Taffy Raphael spent time with Janine and her students during a spring book club session. They were reading *Nana Upstairs and Nana Downstairs* by Tomie dePaola (G.P. Putnam's Sons, 1998) as part of a unit focusing on the role of grandparents in our lives. On the day of one observation, students had read (most of them independently) a page from the story in which dePaola and Nana Upstairs are sitting side by side in her bedroom. Nana is very frail and may be suffering from some form of dementia, although this is not explicitly stated. Instead, dePaola describes how this Nana tells him to "watch out for the fresh one with the hat with the red feather in it. He plays with matches."

As she sends students off to read the page independently, Janine writes a question on the whiteboard, "Who are the little people?" She asks them to think about what they know and what evidence there is in the text for a reader to make sense of what Nana Upstairs is saying. Students are to think about the question and write their thoughts on sticky notes on the page near the spot that prompted their thinking. Taffy and Janine roam the room, looking over students' shoulders as they write. They notice that students have made several predictions, from puppets to ghosts.

Next, Janine asks students to share with a partner who they think the little people are and what they are using to make up their minds. The emphasis is not specifically on QAR but on the knowledge they have about using information sources. The pairs of students share for about five minutes, then Janine asks students to cluster into their book-club groups. Janine drops in on the different groups for a minute or two, for some opportunistic modeling, scaffolding, or explicit instruction. For example, the following interaction illustrates how she uses QAR language to support one student who was using her background knowledge and referring to it with the words "in my head." (Underlines indicate students talking at the same time.)

Jeff: Maybe it's just not really real. It's like just the grandma sees it and Tomie really doesn't.

Janine: Okay.

Jeff: Like it's, it's—

Amanda:	*(interrupting Jeff, who continues talking)* <u>I got another one</u>
Jeff:	—in your head more?
Janine:	Like it's kind of in your head maybe? Briana, I haven't heard from you. What do you think?
Briana:	*(very softly)* I think that it's because, I forgot the right word, Nana is just imagining.
Janine:	She said that maybe Nana is just imagining that. Maybe, okay, keep talking amongst yourselves. I'm going to see how this group is doing, okay?

After Janine has left the group, the students continued to talk and make use of QAR language.

Jamal:	<u>Maybe, uh,</u> someone's using a flashlight to make something appear.
Student 1:	<u>Goooood.</u>
Maya:	That's a good <u>idea,</u>
Student 2:	<u>Maybe—</u>
Maya:	<u>But it's</u> bright out. A flashlight only works in the dark.
Student 3:	<u>Yeah—</u>
Jamal:	<u>Nooo,</u> it can work in the daytime.
Student 2:	Maybe, maybe—
Jamal:	It can make a ghost, too, it can.

(Students bid for the floor.)

Maya:	Maybe it's like, I can talk after Julius. It's kinda like a flash, maybe it's like a flashlight, and you can, 'cause sometimes it's like little flashlight things? Where it makes the little fairy things? You know?
Jamal:	Maybe it's just—
Maya:	—<u>like a ghost!</u>
Nikki:	[inaudible] and it's in their heads, imaginings *(pointing to her head.)*
Jamal:	And how would . . . *(shifting his focus)* Maya! It's like in Cyber Chase. Remember, uh, didn't, uh, they make,

uh, that flashlight, that makes a ghost? That means, it does *(pointing to picture in his book)* make the light.

Maya: You're right.

The goal in Jennifer's and Janine's classrooms is for students to be able to distinguish between the text and the knowledge in their head and then apply this skill not only in their reading lessons but also in settings such as the book discussions above. Expectations for QAR understanding and use rise in subsequent grade levels. You should base your instructional decisions on these expectations and on the levels of knowledge of your students.

Third Grade: Social Studies

Karen Marfise, a colleague of Jennifer's at Shields School, teaches third grade. She faced a set of decisions different from Jennifer's. After the first year of schoolwide QAR instruction, she knew that many of her students would already understand the distinction between In the Book and In My Head QARs. Many of her students would also be able to distinguish between Right There and Think & Search QARs, a focus of teachers in second grade. Therefore, her initial lessons included just a brief review of these concepts.

Following her initial review, and while she was helping her new students to catch up, Karen began to focus lessons on the difference between Author & Me and On My Own. She knew she also had to help her students transform their QAR knowledge by expanding into new

Supporting New Students

To bring students who are new to Shields up to the level of the rest of the class, Karen used time during writers workshop to pull small groups of children together for targeted instruction. During the first few weeks of the school year, she explains the central concepts of In the Book and In My Head to newcomers. During math, science, and reading groups, she uses QAR language and monitors students' levels of understanding by having them talk through the QARs they use for answering particular questions. As soon as they demonstrate that they understand the two sources, she uses similar means to introduce them to the two In the Book QARs. With relatively minimal instruction—and frequent reference to QAR throughout the day—most new students feel comfortable using the language relatively quickly. Of course, the more the language is integrated with the ongoing activities in the school day, the more rapidly new students will develop their understanding.

settings outside of language arts. It was midyear, and all her third graders were completely confident of their ability to distinguish between In the Book and In My Head QARs and had a fairly solid command of the four core categories. She has observed them successfully asking and answering questions across categories. This made her feel comfortable about expanding their use of QAR into other subject areas such as social studies.

Analyzing Artifacts

As part of a social studies unit, Karen has her students analyze artifacts to explore how societies and cultures have changed in the past 100 years. The artifacts include ones from her Swedish grandmother, which she uses as models (see Figure 4.2), as well as artifacts selected by students and their families as representative of their own cultural backgrounds. Using QAR language, she models how to create an extended analysis.

To accompany the model lesson, she gives each student the handout found on page 98. She then teaches a lesson in which she explores how the questions and answers align with the QAR core categories. Students gather around Karen on the carpet area where she has laid out artifacts that had belonged to her grandmother—a flatiron made of cast iron, a metal coffeepot that could be heated on an open fire, a large wooden mortar and pestle, and a washboard. She begins

Figure 4.2 *Using Artifacts as Models*

the lesson by holding up the different objects and asking students to think about what each object might have been used for and why they think that. She asks, "Do you have to use your own ideas to answer the questions on your handout?" As several students nod their heads and murmur yes, she holds an artifact for all to see and asks, "Do you have to see this to answer the questions?" Again, students nod and murmur. Karen then begins to bring in the QAR language, saying, "We have to have two things, right? We have to have the story, but you have to have your brain, too." By holding up the artifact and describing it as a "story," she begins to extend the In the Book and Right There QARs to a very different kind of text.

She then walks the students through the guiding questions on their handout, and they talk about which QAR category each question would represent and what strategies would make sense to use as archaeologists to answer these questions. For example, the first question is a Right There, since all the information is right there in front of them as they look at the object. Students agree that the second question is an Author & Me, so Karen asks them to explain the author part. They suggest that the creator or inventor of the artifact would be the author, and that they would be connecting what they think to the inventor. Karen agrees and says that they need to see the object and consider what they already know in order to figure out how it might have functioned. Similarly, the third question requires knowledge of today's world along with the ability to analyze the artifact. Most students agree that the fifth question is an On My Own, since they could have answered it before they looked at the artifacts. Several, though, point out that the artifacts could help them figure out what has changed, and that would make it an Author & Me.

A similar disagreement happens when they talk about the fourth question. Some students think it could be a Think & Search, since they are using the artifacts to figure out how people lived. Others suggest that the question is an Author & Me, since the objects can't say how they were used. For both the fourth and fifth questions, Karen allows the two perspectives to play out over time, rather than trying to pin down which QAR is the right one. The goal is not to get the QAR right, but to consider the kinds of thinking each QAR elicits. In this case, she is

You Be the Historian

You will examine several artifacts that were found in most homes 100 years ago. Do you know what they are? What do they tell you about the people who used them? How has life changed in the past 100 years? Are there new inventions that have replaced these items, making life easier?

   Pretend you are the archaeologist who discovered these artifacts. You know that they were used in approximately the year 1900. Your job is to figure out what these things were used for and what they tell you about the people who used them.

1. Describe your artifact (shape, size, color, material it is made from).
   Make a drawing to help you remember.

2. What do you think it was used for?

   _____

   _____

3. What might people use today instead of the artifact?

   _____

   _____

4. Does the artifact give you any clue about the way people lived?

   _____

   _____

5. Do you think life is easier or more difficult now than it was 100 years ago? Why?

   _____

   _____

pleased to see the students actively thinking about how the objects could work together to give them insights into people's lives a century ago.

Karen and her students accomplish a great deal in this lesson. By the time they have discussed each question and its connection to QAR, they understand that each object is a kind of text. Further, they have strategies at hand for analyzing the objects, such as visualizing, making text-to-self connections, and making predictions. Each student records his or her ideas on the handout, and then shares them with other students in small groups, much as Janine's students did in their book discussion. With so much opportunity to access appropriate background knowledge, build on one another's ideas, and closely examine the objects/texts, students are very successful at writing extended responses. Their responses take into account what the objects look like, how they may have functioned, and how their functions provide insights into life long ago. Are the objects no longer needed (e.g., mortar and pestle for grinding grain to make bread or cereals), or have they been modernized (e.g., electric steam irons, rather than flatirons heated on an open fire)?

> **You Be the Historian**
>
> You will examine several artifacts that were found in most homes 100 years ago. Do you know what they are? What do they tell you about the people who used them? How has life changed in the past 100 years? Are there new inventions that have replaced these items, making life easier?
>
> Pretend you are the archaeologist who discovered these artifacts. You know that they were used in approximately the year 1900. Your job is to figure out what these things were used for and what they tell you about the people who used them.
>
> 1. Describe your artifact (shape, size, color, material it is made from). Make a drawing to help you remember.
>
> — light brown wood
>
> 2. What do you think it was used for?
> I think it was used for grinding things.
>
> 3. What might people use today instead of the artifact?
> A blender
>
> 4. Does the artifact give you any clue about the way people lived?
> They probably didn't have electricity.
>
> 5. Do you think life is easier or more difficult now than it was 100 years ago? Why?
> It was harder 100 years ago. They didn't have appliances back then.

Sixth Grade: Language Arts and Science

Hannah Natividad, a sixth-grade teacher introduced in Chapter 1, is also a colleague of Jennifer and Karen's. She is responsible for ensuring that her students not only understand the four core QARs but are able to apply them to make sense of increasingly challenging content area textbooks. Further, she knows she will need innovative ways to keep her sixth graders engaged and interacting with one another. For this reason, Hannah often teaches QAR in the context of games that rely on good questioning skills. She makes group-interaction skills central to promote working together across gender lines, social groupings students have formed, language differences, and achievement levels. While students practice QAR skills within these games, Hannah also provides explicit instruction to extend students' QAR knowledge and use in other content subjects.

One game Hannah has created combines a *Jeopardy!*-like format with a book-group discussion. To encourage student interaction, Hannah drew on the concept of "houses" from the popular series about Harry Potter (Gryffindor, Hufflepuff, and so on). At the time we observed her class playing the game, Hannah told us her students were familiar with all core QARs but needed regular opportunities to apply what they had learned in different contexts within the language arts period. With more practice using QAR, they would be ready to extend its use into other subject areas. Hannah begins the questioning game as a whole-class session in which she reviews QAR and introduces the format of the game. Then she points out the game board displayed at the front of the room; it has four rows of six envelopes each. Inside each envelope is a question related to the book the class is reading. Under each envelope, hidden by a flap of paper, is the number of points the question is worth. She explains that they will work within their "houses." A representative from each house sits in one of the chairs Hannah has positioned on the side of the room when it is time for the groups to report to the rest of the class. She has notepaper and markers ready for the groups to use, and she makes sure they all have a copy of the book and their notes.

Next, she explains the rules of the game, and then they begin to play. A representative from one house selects an envelope and hands the question to Hannah, who reads it aloud. Each house gathers to discuss the answer to the question and how they arrived at it (i.e., what source they used). They write down page number(s) and paragraph(s) if they think the question is an In the Book QAR. The representative records the answer and returns to the chair to signal that the group is ready. Hannah tells them that the groups should take at least three or four minutes after they have determined the QAR to review the question and answer to make sure they have the best possible answer. After all groups have shared their responses, the representatives return to the game board to find out how many points their house has earned. Then a representative of the next group selects an envelope to be read aloud.

QAR Now: Question Answer Relationships

The game plays out well. Students converse eagerly, poring over the book for specific information to answer the question. They groan with disappointment when the game ends. Activities such as this one actively engage students, giving them opportunities to use the language of QAR to frame search strategies, draw the necessary inferences, and evaluate the strength of their answers. Moreover, they work in groups that cross social, cultural, ability, and gender differences.

When Hannah feels her students have a solid understanding of QAR categories, she begins to extend their QAR use into other subject areas, such as science. She creates a chart that lists words students can associate with questions within each of the four QAR categories. For example, words like *explain*, *tell why*, and *compare and contrast* tend to (though, of course, not always) signal a Think & Search QAR; *who*, *what*, and *define* tend to signal Right There; words like *form a hypothesis*, *in what ways*, and *solve this* usually indicate a Think & Search question; while words such as *give your own opinion*, *how would you feel if*, and *take a guess* tend to signal

QAR in High School Science

QAR has benefits beyond eighth grade. Jeffrey Wilhelm provides specific ideas about how QAR can help high school students in science. He describes how science teacher Doug Pusey uses Right There questions to foster careful observation and consideration of the available evidence. For example, in a unit that examines what would cause another Ice Age, Doug asks students, "How does the atmosphere behave?" Doug uses Think & Search questions to help students see patterns in the data and to generate inferences and hypotheses about them. In the Ice Age unit, he has students put together information from several news articles about the effects of increased carbon dioxide in the atmosphere and identify patterns. Doug finds that Author & Me questions lead students to generate new hypotheses and theories. Significantly, Author & Me questions promote students' active engagement and personal involvement with science, thus addressing issues of motivation. After having his students read the articles, Doug asks them to develop their own hypotheses about what might happen given different scenarios in the future. Finally, Doug asks On My Own Questions to encourage students to apply scientific concepts to the real world and see how what they have learned can be extended to new contexts. In the Ice Age unit, Doug had students look at real-life effects of increased levels of carbon dioxide and other gases on changes in climate.

Figure 4.3 *Reading/Science Comparison Chart*

READING METHODS	SCIENCE METHODS
On My Own	
1. *Activating Prior Knowledge*—Building upon a topic or issues by determining what you already know and what you want to know.	1. *Making Observations*—Building upon an idea, topic, or issue by observing and determining what you what to know and how it might be changed.
On My Own	
2. *Setting a Purpose*—Turning what you know about a story into a question by asking yourself, "Why am I going to read this story?"	2. *Stating the Question*—Turning what you have observed into a question.
Author & Me	
3. *Predicting*—Stating what you expect to find out in the story.	3. *Stating a Hypothesis*—Stating what you expect to find out in your experiment.
Think & Search	
4. *Reading the Story*— • Skimming to locate main ideas; sequencing the events of the story in chronological order. • Making judgments about the story. • Understanding cause and effect relationships in the story.	4. *Reviewing Literature; Designing an Experiment*— • Skimming the literature to locate the main idea; sequencing the steps of the experiment in chronological order. • Making a judgment about the experimental process. • Understanding the cause or effect of what is being tested.
Right There, Think & Search	
5. *Taking Notes*—Keeping careful records of the story to be able to recall and tell others.	5. *Keeping Data*—Keeping careful records of the experimental data so that it can be repeated and others can see exactly what you did.
Think & Search	
6. *Reading Graphic Aids*—Comparing and contrasting the story, events, characters, and settings in a story (or stories).	6. *Organizing and Analyzing Data*—Comparing and contrasting the experimental data.
Author & Me	
7. *Drawing Conclusions*—Using information from the story to draw conclusions.	7. *Stating a Conclusion*—Using facts and data from the experiment to draw conclusions.
Think & Search	
8. *Writing a Summary*—Recalling the important events in the story.	8. *Writing an Abstract*—Recalling the important events of your experiment.

an On My Own. Having constructed this chart when she was introducing QAR, she continues to refer to it, encouraging students not to simply recognize the types of questions they were asked but also to use their knowledge to generate appropriate questions to promote their own learning across school subjects. Further, in her work with QAR in subject areas such as science, Hannah uses the chart to show them how the language they encounter aligns with the language they are more familiar with in their reading classes (see Figure 4.3). For example, students have learned in language arts classes that On My Own questions require them to activate prior knowledge—to think about what they already know or set a purpose for reading. She links that to QAR in science, showing them how On My Own QARs may use different language but involve the same strategies: When students make an observation, they are activating prior knowledge; when they formulate a question, they are setting a purpose. Similar connections can be seen in Think & Search QARs. Students have learned to take notes to have a careful record of what is happening in a story. In science class, they learn to record data to track what is happening in a science experiment.

Concluding Comments

The lessons Jennifer, Janine, Karen, and Hannah taught illustrate the importance of understanding that there is no one-size-fits-all approach to QAR instruction. Instead, you can use the six-step lesson framework to teach about QAR in myriad ways—from distinguishing between the two information sources to introducing the core QAR categories, from using QAR in the language arts period to using it throughout the school day in different curriculum areas. Jennifer and the others used explicit instruction, review techniques, and even games to introduce students to QAR and to reinforce their use of it. By finding opportunities to engage students with the language and ideas of QAR, you can promote deeper thinking about texts among all students, across grade levels, throughout the school year, and in all subject areas. In the next chapter, we explore how QAR enhances students' ability to perform well on high-stakes tests.

Chapter 5

QAR and Test Preparation

*S*andra Traback, principal of Cesar Chavez Elementary School in Chicago, is keenly aware that high-stakes test scores are used to judge schools' effectiveness. Like many principals, she wants her teachers to be able to provide test preparation that is embedded in high-quality literacy instruction. She wants to avoid having students simply practice test items—taking valuable time away from higher-level instruction in reading comprehension, writing, and other curriculum areas. Sandra asked her primary and intermediate/middle school literacy coordinators, Pat Winger and Rosa Gonzalez, to create a coherent professional development program to meet this goal. Pat, Rosa, and other administrators at Chavez Elementary School developed a plan to extend the professional development on QAR the school had begun earlier in the year to frame the test-preparation focus. They recognized the potential of QAR to help solve the thorny issue of providing relevant test preparation that did not sabotage good literacy instruction.

In this chapter, we focus on how QAR can be used to frame test-preparation activities. First we discuss the limitations of conventional test-prep activities. Second, we present ideas for how QAR can be used to design effective professional development for teachers that results in responsible test-preparation activities embedded within a strong literacy curriculum. Third, we describe how QAR can be used to prepare students for any kind of test question they may encounter–from the day-to-day evaluation activities associated with questions at the end of text passages, stories, chapters, or units to the formal assessments associated with high-stakes tests.

The Limitations of Conventional Test Preparation

Often, test preparation involves having students complete exercises that consist of reading short passages and responding to multiple-choice items. Few commercial test-preparation packages involve having teachers instruct students in higher-level comprehension skills. As Taffy Raphael and Kathryn Au (2005) have noted, students who have not already acquired reading comprehension strategies gain little or nothing from the large amounts of time spent on these conventional test-prep activities. Looking at the results of studies of these kinds of preparation activities, the late Steve Stahl said, "It appears that students are learning how to take tests, not how to think" (Stahl, 2002). Faced with too much of this work, students may actually become anxious about tests or even stop trying to do well on them. Kathy Highfield (2003) interviewed fourth graders who had been engaged in these kinds of activities. When she asked them how they felt about the upcoming state test, students expressed fear, using words such as "scared" and "nervous" or offering comments such as:

* "I feel like I'm gonna fail."
* "It makes me worry."
* "I don't know if I'll get them all right."
* "I worry about how it is going to affect my report card."

Certainly, these students' responses suggest that their test preparation had an effect that was the opposite of what was desired.

More than two decades ago, Taffy Raphael and Clydie Wonnacott (1985) conducted research in which they compared test outcomes for three groups of students: one that had participated in QAR instruction; one that had practiced answering test items; and one that had received regular classroom instruction (the control group). Students in the QAR group performed at higher levels than the students in the other two groups, and Raphael and Wonnacott suggested that the differences in performance reflected QAR's ability to take the mystery out of questioning. Students performed better on their tests when they understood: a) how questions are created, b) the value in drawing on their background knowledge, and c) the need to balance background knowledge with text information. Thus, research suggests that practice-only test preparation may result in test anxiety, and may not boost students' achievement levels.

Professional Development in Support of Responsible Test Preparation

Preparing Students at Every Grade

In states where students are not assessed at each grade (e.g., California, Texas, and Virginia currently test students in third, fifth, and eighth grades), it is still important for the entire school staff to be involved in ensuring that students are prepared. For example, a third-grade exam is designed to assess students' progress up to grade three (i.e., including all that was learned in previous grades as well), so students' success is the responsibility of all teachers through third grade.

In this chapter, we argue for what we characterize as responsible test preparation. Responsible test preparation recognizes the dilemma that most teachers face today. Not only are students evaluated on the basis of their performance on high-stakes tests, so too are schools, districts, and teachers. This reality necessarily informs curriculum and instructional decisions teachers make. For example, teachers may feel they must take time away from ongoing literacy instruction to have students practice items similar to those on the test (much like Kathy Highfield's colleagues were asked to do). Yet teachers cannot ignore their responsibility to ensure that students have the strategies they need to succeed in test settings.

We believe QAR instruction can serve as the basis of responsible test preparation. Teaching students about QAR demystifies how tests work and helps students become highly accustomed to the language of these tests. QAR instruction should be based on a deep understanding of the content the tests will cover and the strategies students need to do well. In addition, students should be taught strategies in a way that allows them to build on what they are learning year after year.

Understanding How Content Is Tested

A starting point for creating a responsible approach to test preparation is to focus on how the content of the state's standards is tested at each grade level by studying the released items from past state tests. For example, Texas releases items from the Texas Assessment of Knowledge and Skills (TAKS) to the general public each year, posting them on the state board of education's Web site for anyone to download. Figure 5.1 shows how the standards correspond to the released items, as well as the question numbers that correspond to each standard.

The analysis displayed in Figure 5.1 shows how the TAKS attempts to measure learning in specific content areas. By focusing at the level of the standard, teachers can create instructional approaches that will help students regardless of the specific format a test item might take. For example, the first standard in Figure 5.1 states,

> Draw on experiences to bring meanings to words in context such as interpreting figurative language and multiple meaning words.

To demonstrate their command of this standard, students will need to understand figurative language and make inferences about what the figurative language means. They have to draw on the text context (information provided by the author) and their own interpretation of what the author is trying to suggest by words that cannot be taken literally (information the reader provides). The teacher understands that students will have to recognize that even familiar words may have

Figure 5.1 **Analysis of TAKS Fourth-Grade English Language Arts Released Test Items and State Standards**

Standard	Question Number
4.9B	8 30

Draw on experiences to bring meanings to words in context such as interpreting figurative language and multiple meaning words.

Standard	Question Number
4.10E	13 20 39

Use text structure to create and recall information.

4.10F   1   4   5   10   12   17   18   21   25   33   37   40
Determine main idea and supporting ideas.

4.10G   15
Paraphrase and summarize text to recall, inform, and organize ideas.

4.10H   2   6   7   9   11   27   32   36
Draw inferences/conclusions to make generalizations with supporting evidence.

4.10I   28
View similarities and differences across texts.

4.10L   3   26
Represent text information using outline, timeline, graphic organizer.

4.11C   31   35
Support responses by using own experiences and model how to connect, compare, and contrast ideas across texts.

4.12A   24
Recognize that authors organize information in specific ways.

4.12H   14   16   19   23   29   34   38
Analyze character traits, points of view, motivations, conflicts, relationships, changes they undergo.

4.12I   22
Recognize and analyze story plot, setting, and problem resolution.

multiple meanings—an Author & Me QAR. When instruction focuses on the knowledge underlying the standard—in this case, understanding figurative language and interpreting the appropriate meaning for a word—rather than simply practicing a particular test-item format, students will be better prepared to handle a range of assessments, including multiple-choice questions, short-answer items, and more extended responses.

The analysis shown in Figure 5.1 also provides a clear picture of the distribution of questions across the standards. That is, some standards may have many questions attached to them while other standards may have only a few. Using the TAKS analysis as an example, a glance at Figure 5.1 shows that one standard (4.10F—*Determine main idea and supporting ideas*) has far more questions on the examination than any of the others, while standard (4.10G—*Paraphrase and summarize text to recall, inform, and organize ideas*) has only one item. Although distribution of questions across standards may vary from year to year, doing this kind of analysis across the years will give you a clearer sense of the trends and patterns within your state.

Test Items and QAR Categories

In an analysis of released test items from several state tests, we found that each test item could be placed into one of the core QAR categories. Figure 5.2 shows a sample of the analyses from four state tests: California (CST), Florida (FCAT), Texas (TAKS), and Virginia (VSLA).

From the table, it is evident that Think & Search and Author & Me are the two most prevalent QAR types your students are likely to encounter. This is encouraging, in that authentic reasons for reading involve making connections within a text as well as between what we read and our own experiences. However, it is best not to limit your instruction just to the most common categories; QAR instruction can be used to show students other categories they will encounter and what form they take.

Figure 5.2 *Analysis of State Test Items and QARs*

State Test—English Language Arts or the Equivalent	Grade	QAR Right There	QAR Think & Search	QAR Author & Me	QAR On My Own
California Standards Test (CST)	3	3	5	13	11
	5	1	8	15	14
	8	2	10	15	11
Florida Comprehensive Assessment Test (FCAT)	-	-	-	-	-
	4	2	5	8	0
	8	2	8	6	0
Texas Assessment of Knowledge & Skills (TAKS)	3	13	25	33	1
	5	2	19	12	0
	8	4	18	26	0
Virginia Standards of Learning Assessment (VSLA)	3	2	5	11	7
	5	2	7	23	2
	8	1	11	30	0

For example, on the California Standards Test, or CST, there were a number of questions within the On My Own QAR category, testing students' general knowledge, such as:

Which word below rhymes with <u>boat</u>?

a. fleet   c. note

b. nose   d. bow

Students must use their knowledge of rhyming in order to answer this question; that the passage content is about a boating trip is irrelevant. Students will need instruction to see that this is a classic example of a test question that appears to be an In the Book QAR when, in fact, it does not require the reader to have read the text at all. Rather, the QAR is an On My Own requiring knowledge of variations in how long /o/ can be spelled.

Becoming Familiar With How Questions Are Evaluated

A second aspect of becoming familiar with the alignment of state tests to standards focuses on making the scoring systems visible across grade levels. Most states release sample items, associated rubrics, and anchor texts—samples of answers deemed acceptable—so there are no mysteries regarding the knowledge, skills, and strategies students will be expected to apply in answering the more open-ended test items. These rubrics list specific strategies and skills that students must use, whether information in an extended response comes from the student's own knowledge base (i.e., On My Own QARs) or from information derived from a combination of text and background knowledge (i.e., Author & Me). The anchor texts also show how much detail students will be expected to provide—and whether the details must come from the text as well as their own experiences.

Chavez Elementary: Professional Development in Action

The analyses described above are central to ensuring you are armed with the knowledge you need to embed test preparation within a strong literacy curriculum. In this section, we return to Chavez Elementary to take a look at the professional development plan the literacy coordinators, Pat and Rosa, developed. Their three-phase model provides one example of how a school staff moved from test-analysis activities to literacy instruction designed to both support students' test-taking and ensure they were developing key literacy strategies they would need across all subject areas.

Phase I: Analyzing QARs

In Phase I of the Chavez model, the teachers met in grade-level teams to look at the Learning First tests—the district-mandated school-wide assessments in reading—designed for their grade level.

Figure 5.3 *Discussion Guide*

Directions for Use in Grade-Level and Whole-School Discussions

- Distribute the text and questions appropriate to the grade-level grouping (e.g., a single grade-level would require that all fifth grade teachers be given the fifth grade materials; grade-level clusters such as "intermediate" would require that all teachers in the cluster be given all tests and questions relative to those in the grouping, such as for grades 3–5).

- Provide the attached "QAR Test Analysis Chart" and explain that the teachers in the grade level will be examining the Learning First materials to analyze the strategies students would have to know to be successful in responding to each question.

- Ask all participants to read the passage and answer each question.

- When everyone has had a chance to do the task, lead a discussion for each question examining what QAR they believe it to best represent and the strategies that students would need to know to answer it correctly.

- When each grade-level grouping has had a chance to discuss this, ask teachers in the grade level to make a master list of the strategies their students will be expected to use successfully.

- In a whole-school discussion, lay out the QARs students will be expected to handle and, for each QAR, the strategies the students will need. Use this discussion as a first step to creating a "staircase curriculum" that will ensure a coherent literacy instructional focus across grade levels so that

  - students see consistent language being used within and across grade levels in terms of the QAR categories and the "names" given to the strategies within each category;

  - teachers use QAR to frame the language so students learn strategies that "go together" and strategies that help with different kinds of questions;

  - strategy knowledge builds from the beginning to the end of the year and from early to later grades.

QAR Now: Question Answer Relationships

Their goal was to analyze the patterns of the QARs reflected in each test. Then they shared their analysis with other grade-level teams. Figure 5.3, Discussion Guide and Figure 5.4, QAR Test Analysis Chart are the materials they used in Phase I.

Figure 5.4 *QAR Test Analysis Chart*

Question #	Answer	QAR Used	Comprehension Strategy That Facilitates Answering the Question
1			
2			
3			
4			
5			
6			
7			
8			
9			
10			
11			
12			
13			

On a Friday morning in early November, faculty and staff gathered in the school library. After briefly reviewing QAR, Pat asked each grade-level team to take its grade level's assessment test and analyze the questions in terms of the QAR category they represent. Each team then created a summary chart displaying how the QARs on the assessment were distributed (Figure 5.5 illustrates the analysis for the first few questions by the fourth-grade team).

Figure 5.5 **QAR Analysis Chart for the Fourth-Grade Test: Phase I**

Question #	Answer	QAR Used	Comprehension Strategy That Facilitates Answering the Question
1	B	Author & Me	
2	C	Author & Me	
3	D	On My Own	
4	B	Author & Me	
5	C	Think & Search	
6	A	Right There or Think & Search	

The meeting ended with the grade levels sharing what they had found and creating a chart that showed the QARs emphasized at each grade level. The staff noticed that across the grade levels, most questions represented Think & Search and Author & Me QARs. A few Right There QARs, which asked students to identify an important detail from the selection, were present on each test. The few On My Own QARs were primarily related to word meanings (e.g., students could choose the appropriate definition without having to read the story) or punctuation (e.g., students could select the appropriate punctuation mark without having understood the story). This work set up the second phase of the professional development activity.

Phase II: Identifying Comprehension Strategies

To prepare for the second phase of the professional development program, teachers met in grade-level teams to identify comprehension

Figure 5.6 *QAR Analysis Chart for the Fourth-Grade Test: Phase II*

Question #	Answer	QAR Used	Comprehension Strategy That Facilitates Answering the Question
1	B	Author & Me	Making inferences • Integrating story evidence • Applying word knowledge (using known vocabulary in new context) Identifying important information Summarizing • Comparing
2	C	Author & Me	Making inferences (from story evidence) Sequencing (understanding temporal relations)
3	D	On My Own	Using background knowledge (about text genres)
4	B	Author & Me	Identifying important information Understanding theme/purpose
5	C	Think & Search	Making inferences • Visualizing • Using context clues
6	A	Right There or Think & Search	Skimming Summarizing within a single paragraph

strategies their students would need to use to answer each QAR at their grade level successfully. Each team created a chart—this time focusing on the strategies useful for each of the QARs students would likely face (see Figure 5.6 for the beginning of the fourth-grade team's chart).

At a second school-wide professional development meeting, each grade-level team presented what it had found to the rest of the staff. Pat and Rosa collected the charts from each team and, together with the staff, created a school-wide profile detailing the comprehension strategies students needed to know at each grade level. They organized the strategies within the QAR categories. Thus, in their school, students would learn—year after year—not only different strategies that could help them with particular question answer relationships but how to connect and use the strategies effectively in a variety of situations, including high-stakes tests.

Phase III: Planning for Teaching the Strategies

To prepare for the third phase of the professional development plan, Pat and Rosa distributed a short text to each grade-level team. In grade-level meetings, teachers shared ideas about how they would teach their students various strategies that seemed relevant given the students' performance on the mandated test as well as their day-to-day work during literacy instruction (e.g., guided reading, book club discussions). As a team they decided on one strategy to model for the

Paying Attention to Text Levels

In Chicago, Taffy Raphael has been working with several schools in a collaborative endeavor among the university, the public schools, and a community philanthropic organization. Some of the participating schools in the project, Partnership READ, have focused on creating a coherent, school-wide literacy curriculum using QAR. Several of the schools extended that work to create a coherent, responsible test-preparation approach similar to the one at Chavez Elementary.

Some of the teachers in Partnership READ made an interesting discovery. In the initial stages of developing a test-preparation approach they focused on developing a deeper knowledge of tests such as the Iowa Test of Basic Skills (ITBS), the Illinois State Achievement Test (ISAT), and their district's new Learning First test, since these are the types of tests on which they and their students are judged. In two of the schools, the literacy coordinators downloaded sample passages from the ITBS and ISAT and distributed them to teachers, leaving off all identifying information for the grade level of the test passages. During a series of faculty meetings, staff members took the tests and met in small groups to talk about the task demands associated with each passage and its related question.

Most of the teachers were surprised at how consistently they had overestimated the grade level of the passages based on text difficulty. That is, a third-grade passage was often assumed to be a fifth- or sometimes eighth-grade passage. This was a very helpful activity in terms of alerting teachers to the possible need to raise the level of their instructional focus and their expectations over the year so students would not be surprised by the passages on the tests. Without such analysis, teachers might not expose their students to texts with enough complexity, length, or difficulty to prepare them adequately for the test.

rest of the staff, using the passage that Pat and Rosa had distributed. In this way, teachers across grade levels were able to see a developmental progression for how a particular strategy was taught.

For example, summarizing is central to answering Think & Search QARs in each grade level, but the specific strategies used vary across grade levels. Kindergarten teachers modeled a retelling strategy; eighth-grade teachers modeled a synthesizing strategy that involved providing supporting evidence for a theme they identified.

Certainly, much of these analyses and sharing session opportunities could be created outside the realm of QAR language. But using QAR as the organizing framework helped the teachers create a consistent language, and it made the connections among strategies more visible to students, even across subject areas and grade levels.

Using QAR to Explore the Task Demands of Tests With Students

Armed with a good sense of the text difficulty and the standards that the questions on a test are designed to assess, you can comfortably turn to examining specific questions to determine the task demands they place on students. Students generally encounter two types of questions on tests: multiple-choice and open-ended. QAR can help students see how to draw on relevant knowledge sources for both of these question types.

Multiple-Choice Questions

Multiple-choice tests are designed with *foils*—that is, tempting responses that only partially answer a question and therefore are incorrect. Students taking high-stakes tests should not count on easily eliminating foils. Instead, you need to help them understand what to do when there are four reasonable choices and they must choose the best answer. For example, a typical third-grade reading subtest may ask students to read the poem "Monday" and answer the question that follows it.

> ## Monday
>
> I overslept and missed my bus.
> I didn't have time to eat.
> I wore plaid pants with polka dots
> And my sneakers on the wrong feet.
> I trudged to school in the rain
> And got there just in time
> To hear the teacher announce a test
> On math chapters one through nine.
> When teacher asked if we had questions,
> I raised my hand and said,
> "I'm not quite ready for today.
> May I please go back to bed?"

1. **What is this poem mainly about?**

    (a) **Walking in the rain**

    (b) **Having a bad day**

    (c) **Taking a math test**

    (d) **Dressing in plaid pants**

Using their knowledge of QAR, students will consider both the question and the answer together. The question asks what the poem is "mainly about," signaling that the information is most likely to be found in the text (a reader wouldn't know what a text is about if they hadn't read it). However, poems rarely have lines that read, "This poem is mainly about. . ." so it may not be a Right There QAR.

Instead, they will need to use Think & Search QAR strategies—putting information together, visualizing what the poem is describing, and so forth—to make the final decision. In fact, (b) "Having a bad day" is the only answer that takes into account the information in all the lines of the poem. Knowing that Think & Search QARs often ask them to provide either main ideas or details to support an answer, students can be confident that Think & Search strategies will guide them to identify the best response.

Let's look at a second question related to the poem that illustrates how the format—multiple choice—can be used for Right There QARs. In this sample, the table of contents of the book in which the poem appears is the source of the information for answering the question. Students must read this text, but not the poem itself, to choose the best answer. In fact, the poem's title is a distracter that could mislead a careless reader. The directions state:

Read this part of a table of contents. Use it to answer the next two questions.

Sun and Moon 10

On Your Way 12

Math Tests 14

At the Beach 16

Monday 18

Saturday Morning 20

2. Which poem begins on page 12?

(a) "On Your Way"

(b) "Monday"

(c) "Sun and Moon"

(d) "Saturday Morning"

To determine the QAR for this test item, students must read the table of contents, find page 12, and look directly next to it to see that the poem on page 12 is titled "On Your Way." This is a clear example of a question that requires Right There QAR strategies such as skimming or scanning, described in Chapter 3. The answer is clearly stated in the text. Knowing that Right There QARs have the answer right on the page will help guide students to choose an appropriate strategy for answering this question. In a test situation students should not waste time rereading the poem to answer this question, nor should they want to be confused by the title of the poem they had read, when the question is not asking about the poem.

A third question following "Monday" illustrates how In My Head QARs can be used strategically to answer even a multiple-choice question. The question asks:

3. **At the end of the poem, the person speaking feels—**

    (a) **Excited**

    (b) **Happy**

    (c) **Nervous**

    (d) **Frustrated**

In this case, students can skim the poem or simply remember that it did not state how the poet felt. Students who know QAR will know immediately that this means they must use the poem and their heads, a classic Author & Me QAR. Students must consider the phrases the poet uses to capture what he or she is thinking about and then draw on their own experiences to think about how these phrases are likely to make someone feel. They may note that many of the descriptions in the poem express frustration, leading them to select (d) "Frustrated" as the best response.

This fourth multiple-choice question following the poem illustrates how On My Own QAR strategies can be helpful with some questions. This question asks,

4. **Which words in the poem name PEOPLE, PLACES, or THINGS?**

    (a) **to, in, on**

    (b) **missed, trudged, raised**

    (c) **bus, feet, rain**

    (d) **a, the, my**

Here the item is designed to determine if students know which of the four choices contains nouns. Students can easily answer this question by just looking at the choices given. They do not need to read the entire poem to do so—something students will recognize as an On My Own QAR.

QAR is a powerful tool for taking the mystery out of multiple-choice questions. At the same time, it demonstrates clearly to students that they should not make simple assumptions, such as thinking multiple-choice questions always reflect In the Book QAR categories. Again, the language of QAR provides you and your students with a way to unpack the task demands and link them to appropriate comprehension strategies for identifying the best answers. As we shall see, similar benefits can be found in helping students analyze open-ended questions, whether short answer or extended response.

Open-ended Questions

Open-ended questions require students to form a complete answer that effectively communicates their thinking in a clear and concise manner and uses details from the text to support their response. Open-ended questions can appear in a variety of forms, so it is important that you check your state education department Web site to better understand how open-ended questions are used to assess students. The following open-ended question is a released item from the Florida Comprehensive Assessment Test (2001). The question refers to a passage, from "The Bell of Atri," a story retold by James Baldwin, and is one of the two open-ended ones that accompany this text. In most states, an answer sheet accompanies each released item. This answer sheet sometimes includes the rubric that was used to score students' responses, as well as anchor texts. Both are used to train the official state scorers and show teachers, as well as the general public, the rubrics and the expectations for students' writing.

Here is the first sample question and answer related to "The Bell of Atri":

> How does the knight's treatment of his horse relate to the lesson of the story? Use details and information from the story to support your answer.

The state included the following to indicate an acceptable response:

> The knight's treatment of a horse relates to the lesson of the story: Justice and fair treatment should be available to all. At first, the knight's horse was his loyal companion who served him well, and the knight treated him well. After the knight grew older, all he cared about was gold, neglecting and ill treating his horse, finally turning it out. When the hungry horse nibbled on the grapevine rope, it accidentally alerted the judges to its mistreatment. For example, one of the judges said that everyone knew the knight treated his horse shamefully. The horse, in the end, got justice—good food and shelter. The lesson of this story is that justice should be available to everyone, and everyone should be treated fairly—even a horse.

The above question asks students to understand the lesson of the story and then to compare the treatment of one of the characters (the horse) to that lesson. Since the lesson is not explicitly stated in the story, students will need to consider strategies related to Author & Me. They will need both to have read and understood important information from the text and to infer the actual lesson to be learned (i.e., come from their heads). However, the second part of the question asks for supporting information from the text, clearly signaling students to return to the text to identify key ideas. Here they may draw on Think & Search strategies, looking across the key ideas in the text to include all the relevant reasons. Simply going to a single point in the text using Right There strategies will not provide a substantive enough response to receive an acceptable score.

You can use samples such as the question above to lead students to recognize the multipart question and to realize that they may need to draw on their knowledge of more than one QAR to answer it. Using only one QAR would provide only a partial answer. Understanding this complexity is particularly important for older students who are dealing with more difficult text. Because open-ended questions require students to build an argument based on an inference or a conclusion, this can also increase the risk for students. If their first conclusion is incorrect, their argument may be built on false ground. You can help students see how the sections of an answer can be used to make sure they are building a strong answer. If their details do not support their inference very well, they may need to revisit their initial inference and revise it.

Open-ended questions can be quite complex. Sharing sample questions and related rubrics with students, particularly when linked to their QAR knowledge, can provide all students with an advantage. Further, when such analysis is part of the ongoing, rich literacy environment of their classroom, students will become confident and ready to apply what they have been learning, even under the stress of a high-stakes test setting.

Concluding Comments

A classroom culture that supports and includes QAR is not only helping students become the best test takers possible, but is also doing so in a responsible manner. Kathy Highfield used QAR rather than a district-mandated practice-test approach with her class and discovered several advantages, including QAR's efficiency. The practice-test approach consumed nearly 50 hours of instructional time over a three-month period, more than double the 18 hours of time students spent focusing on tests in the QAR classrooms. Typical QAR lessons involve students in writing questions, engaging in student-to-student talk, learning and practicing reading comprehension strategies as part of daily work, and building positive attitudes toward testing. When asked how they felt about an upcoming test, her students responded: "It's okay," "I'm not that scared of it," and "I feel comfortable."

In a QAR classroom, teachers model and coach students, moving students toward independence. Treating test preparation as an inherent part of education and tests as a format to be studied and learned will benefit students and allow you to better manage this sometimes overwhelming task. A state's Web site is a rich source of information that can help you better prepare your students for test taking. The main goal in QAR is to develop a classroom culture in which deep thinking is the norm and students have opportunities to work with texts written for their age levels. Thus, when high-stakes tests come, students are well equipped to succeed and move on to their next challenge.

Chapter 6

The Benefit of Whole-School Adoption of QAR

*R*ita Gardner, principal at Shields Elementary School, contacted Taffy Raphael in late spring to invite her to work with her staff on Question Answer Relationships the following year. Rita was proud of her school—a neighborhood school in one of Chicago's high-poverty settings, serving primarily Latino children—and the progress her pre-school through middle school teachers had made. However, she had two concerns: the lack of progress the students at Shields had made in using comprehension strategies in their day-to-day classroom work and their reading scores on the state standardized test given in third, fifth, and eighth grades. She believed every teacher, not just teachers at those grade levels, was responsible for ensuring that students were successful. She wanted her teaching staff to focus their instruction on high-level thinking and, at the same time, help prepare students for high-stakes tests. And she wanted to do this in a meaningful way, one that would unite a staff that was responsible for teaching more than 1,000 students located in three different buildings. She believed QAR was the answer.

Working collaboratively, Taffy and the classroom teachers set goals for what they wanted to accomplish at each grade level so that students' knowledge about QAR would build over the years. Teachers used QAR to organize comprehension instruction so that students heard a common vocabulary across school subjects and across grade levels. They worked to ensure that students in bilingual classrooms heard the same terms and engaged in strategy application in ways that paralleled the mainstream classrooms. At the end of the year, in an e-mail to Taffy, Rita noted the benefits of QAR for her teachers. They had

* developed a common language for comprehension instruction;
* talked about their professional activities—sharing across subject areas and across grade levels.

Her students had

* gained confidence in different academic situations;
* boosted their test-taking performances.

In previous chapters we have focused primarily on how individual teachers can apply QAR in the classroom to improve their students' reading comprehension. In this chapter, we share our experience in working with several schools that have adopted QAR on a schoolwide basis. First, we present the background underlying a whole-school approach to change. Second, we describe the steps a school can take to use QAR on a schoolwide basis. Third, we describe the potential impact on teachers and students of QAR use throughout a school.

Background About Whole-School Change

Teachers at many schools have told us that they are tired of working hard on one school improvement initiative after another, only to find that these initiatives end up having little or no effect on students' literacy achievement. Typically, initiatives fail for a number of reasons—often the majority of teachers have not bought into them, or they are too complex and cumbersome to be sustained over time, or they do not connect to a systematic long-term plan for school improvement. Using QAR as a schoolwide framework for improving student achievement—initially in literacy blocks and later in other school subjects—potentially can be a way of surmounting these obstacles.

Any school successful with schoolwide change based on QAR or other concepts must have certain elements already in place, and good leadership is certainly one of these elements. At Shields Elementary, Rita Gardner provided strong leadership for the implementation of QAR across all classrooms. Jean Nielsen, the school's literacy coordinator, worked closely with Rita. She was responsible for managing the process on a day-to-day basis. Elsewhere, we have written about how improving reading achievement through a schoolwide effort requires strong leadership, particularly in terms of coordinating curriculum change across the grade levels (Au, 2006). Jean also saw it as her job to maintain a focus on QAR from kindergarten through eighth grade, so that there would be a coherent curriculum for reading comprehension. Through the professional development workshops and discussions on QAR that she facilitated, teachers developed a common language about comprehension as well as confidence that they were teaching in ways that met their students' needs.

Involve All Teachers

The best approach is for a school to involve all teachers with QAR instruction right from the beginning. Sometimes administrators tell us that they want to start by having just a handful of teachers begin working with QAR in their classrooms. These teachers may be volunteers or they may be handpicked because they are the doers, the ones who are willing to try something new. The logic of going with the doers is that these teachers' triumphs will inspire other teachers to try QAR. Although they will almost certainly find success with QAR in their own classrooms, there are several reasons why this approach to changing school practice is less likely to have long-term benefits than one involving everyone from the beginning (Au, 2006). One reason is that the school's faculty becomes immediately divided into doers and bystanders, and a natural attitude of bystanders is to remain indifferent and treat the innovation as someone else's responsibility. Another reason is that going with the doers signals that administration has decided not to confront the issues that may be dividing the faculty. Avoiding important discussions that lead to coherent school practices makes it more difficult to bring about long-term changes.

We strongly recommend involving all teachers with QAR from the beginning, including teachers working with English-language learners and special education students, as well as paraprofessional aides who may be tutoring individuals or small groups of students. Students who need additional help will especially benefit from the consistency across settings and will be better able to apply what they are learning in one setting to other parts of their school day.

Getting Teacher Buy-In

In our experience, lack of teacher buy-in can be a key obstacle to whole-school efforts. On the one hand, administrators and teachers generally agree on the need to improve students' literacy learning, especially in schools that are located in high-poverty areas and serving large numbers of students of diverse cultural and linguistic backgrounds. These schools often have low reading test scores, and the teachers are under heavy pressure from the district to make changes that raise scores. On the other hand, while they may embrace the need for change, teachers may be leery of making a commitment to a reform effort, and for good reason. Most schools in high-poverty areas have already been through a number of different initiatives that, singly or cumulatively, have not led to improved results. These initiatives often have been extremely costly not just in terms of dollars spent for training and materials but in terms of teachers' time and energy.

QAR has proved successful in generating schoolwide teacher buy-in because it provides one of the few frameworks teachers can immediately recognize as being useful for students from kindergarten through high school. For example, in Chicago, where many teachers work in K–8 schools, it can be difficult to find an initiative that addresses the central concerns of all the teachers. A reform effort that focuses on beginning reading may have little relevance or appeal to teachers at grade 4 and above, while one that emphasizes adolescent literacy may not be compelling to those who teach in the primary grades. QAR, with its emphasis on higher-level thinking with text, can lead teachers to common points of discussion because comprehension is a concern for all teachers. As shown in earlier chapters, the two basic QAR categories, In My Head and In the Book, can be introduced easily to kindergarten and first-grade children, while the complexities of Author & Me and Think & Search questions can provide food for thought through high school and beyond.

QAR: Easy to Understand, Easy to Implement

Another strength of QAR as the basis for schoolwide change is that it is easy for teachers to understand and teach. Though QAR is not without its subtleties and complexities, its basic concepts are entirely straightforward. In our experience, the most challenging aspect for teachers is getting accustomed to using the terminology of the four QARs: Right There, Think & Search, On My Own, and Author & Me. Referring to the language of QAR, one teacher told us, "At first I felt like I just couldn't get the words out, and I had to get to the point where the words came out of my mouth automatically." After the first couple of lessons, this teacher found that the language of QAR did become automatic for her. Once teachers feel comfortable with the language, they find it easy to teach QAR lessons and to bring QAR into classroom discussions in a systematic way.

Also, it's not necessary to develop a new school or classroom schedule. QAR instruction fits right into many existing curricula.

Furthermore, the time and expense required for a school to get started with QAR is minimal. Typically, a half-day workshop gives teachers enough background to begin working with QAR in their classrooms. Follow-up meetings can be helpful, especially for teachers in the same grade level or department to discuss how they are teaching QAR and to monitor students' progress. Though commercially available materials can be used to make QAR instruction even easier (e.g., Raphael & Au, 2001), teachers can readily create QAR lessons based on texts already available in their classrooms (Raphael & Au, 2005). As suggested in earlier chapters, teachers can base QAR lessons on passages from novels; textbooks for math, science, and social studies; and newspapers and magazines.

Quick Results

Finally, QAR helps to win teacher buy-in and commitment to whole-school change because it shows quick results. Milagros Vazzano, a third-grade bilingual transitional teacher at Shields School in Chicago, described how one of her colleagues had asked her for help with QAR. The two traded classes so that Milagros could introduce QAR to the other teacher's students. The next day, the other teacher thanked Milagros for helping her students gain confidence in answering questions. She said that the class was reading a text with accompanying questions when one boy held up his hand and yelled, "Right There!" The boy explained that the question had a Right There answer and shared the answer. Teachers at many schools have told us that for the time and effort spent, QAR provides a substantial payoff in terms of students' learning, and in the end, it is results that motivate teachers to continue with QAR.

The Process of Whole-School Change

We find that the systematic process of whole-school change can be broken down to five broad phases of teacher work.

1. Understanding the big picture of reading

2. Setting goals for student learning

3. Monitoring student progress

4. Reporting results to the whole school

5. Improving instruction

The approach described below is an application of the Standards-Based Change Process, which is described in more detail by Kathryn Au (2006) and Au, Hirata, and Raphael (2005).

1. Understanding the Big Picture of Reading and QAR

Helping teachers understand the big picture of reading sets the context for working with QAR as the basis for whole-school change. That big picture comprises two key concepts, as discussed in Chapter 1. Teachers and students must be prepared to address ambitious standards of literacy that emphasize higher-level thinking with text, not just lower-level recall, and teachers must recognize the gap between the literacy achievement of students of diverse cultural and linguistic backgrounds and their mainstream peers.

It may be useful to hold a workshop or study session in which teachers read and discuss Chapter 1 or articles with similar content (e.g., Raphael & Au, 2005). Such sessions can be conducted by the teachers themselves or led by the school's curriculum coordinator, a university consultant, or another reading expert. The facilitator can begin by making connections to state or district reading standards, which frequently are modeled on the NAEP and have a similar emphasis on comprehension and higher-level thinking. As we described in Chapter 5, we have found that teachers may not be aware of the extent to which expectations for students' performance levels as readers have risen. These teachers may be teaching lower-level forms of reading comprehension, such as story elements or the sequence of events, but not developing their students' ability to reason with text. Once teachers become aware of the importance of higher-level thinking with text, they will recognize the value of QAR.

Teachers need to be able to make the connections between the two key concepts—higher-level thinking with text and the literacy achievement gap—and their own school setting. They generally recognize the importance of analyzing the school's reading achievement results. At Shields, for example, teachers at each grade level looked at relevant results from the two high-stakes tests and at anecdotal information they shared about their students' performance levels during reading and content area lessons.

When doing these kinds of analyses, it's important to consider issues of equity. At many schools, students from low-income families and English-language learners have lower test results than other students. In our experience, taking a hard look at students' present levels of reading achievement almost always points to the need to improve reading comprehension instruction. Teachers usually conclude that they need to place a greater emphasis on reading comprehension instruction across the board, and that they must attend in particular to providing reading comprehension instruction to certain subgroups of students, such as English-language learners, who may have received little such instruction in the past.

When teachers understand the big picture, it's much easier for them to see the value of QAR as the basis for a whole-school initiative. As we mentioned earlier, a half-day workshop provides adequate time to present teachers with the big picture and provide background on QAR. Introducing teachers to QAR follows the same approach used with students. The facilitator begins by laying out the distinction between In the Book and In My Head and then unpacks the four core categories, using the illustrations and definitions described in Chapter 1.

Teachers benefit from the opportunity to apply what they have learned immediately—for example, by generating questions for a common text, followed by small-group activities in which teachers answer the question and discuss the QAR category. These discussions highlight the point that often—depending on how they have answered the question and how much background knowledge they had on the topic—what is an

In the Book QAR for one reader may be an On My Own for another. Such discussions should also helps emphasize the importance of keeping the focus for QAR on supporting students' thinking and on helping them learn to justify the rationale for an answer, rather than on figuring out the "right" QAR.

2. Setting Goals for Student Learning

Once teachers have become familiar with the big picture of reading and the basics of QAR, they are ready for the second phase in the whole-school process: setting goals for student learning. The first step is to develop a vision statement that describes the excellent reader who graduates from the school. The statement establishes an endpoint for a coherent reading comprehension curriculum across the grades (Newmann, Smith, Allenworth, & Bryk, 2001). A coherent curriculum can be visualized as a staircase (as shown in Figure 6.1). Teachers at

Figure 6.1 *A Staircase Curriculum*

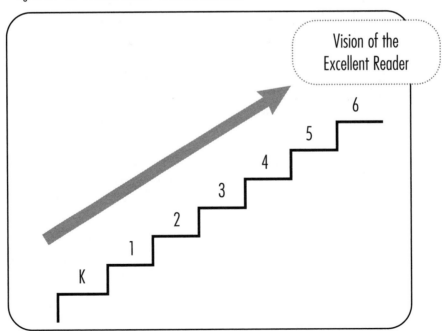

each grade level understand the expectations for students in the subsequent grade and what they need to do to prepare students for the next year's work.

This curriculum is somewhat different from the spiral curriculum that has been accepted as conventional wisdom for many years. In a spiral, ideas are revisited—a concept that, unfortunately, can be interpreted as the need to simply reteach similar concepts across the grade levels. The assumption that if children aren't successful in one grade, they can pick up what they have missed in the next, can leave children behind. The staircase emphasizes achieving end-of-year goals every year, so that children are prepared to continue upward, toward high-level, end-of-schooling targets. Creating a vision of the graduate of the school—what he or she should know and be able to do—helps teachers at each grade level consider their contribution to achieving it.

In defining this ideal graduate, the teachers bring into the discussion what they know about rising standards for literacy achievement and the importance of higher-level thinking with text. For example, teachers at a school in Hawaii agreed on the following vision statement:

> The successful reader who leaves our school will be able to read with a clear purpose, engage in an ongoing process of questioning to understand big concepts and generalizations, and continue to apply and make connections.

Notice the emphasis on higher-level thinking with text, including generalizations and making connections. The vision statement at Shields shares similar high-level goals:

> Shields students will be able to ask good questions, think critically, and make connections that help make sense of text to improve reading comprehension in order to become successful readers.

Teachers at all grade levels relate their work to the vision statement they have helped create. Because many schools in Chicago, like Shields, enroll students from kindergarten through eighth grade, their vision statements describe a graduating eighth grader. Knowing what they are trying to accomplish as a school community, the kindergarten, first-, and second-grade teachers orient their reading instruction toward this same vision. The vision statement unifies reading instruction across the entire school.

Establish Grade-Level Benchmarks

The next step is for all the teachers to determine what they must accomplish at their own grade levels. Teachers should develop grade-level benchmarks, or end-of-year outcomes, based on what they believe their grade level should contribute to the staircase curriculum shown in Figure 6.1. The benchmarks are based on their experience, as well as on their knowledge of state standards, scope and sequence of skills and strategies from their reading program, district guidelines, and so forth.

Kindergarten teachers strive to move students to the top of the first step in the staircase curriculum, first-grade teachers take them to the second step, and second-grade teachers take them to the third step, and so on. When QAR is used as the basis for whole-school change, teachers at each grade level discuss what students at each grade level should know and be able to do with QAR to improve their reading comprehension. The information presented in chapters 1 and 4 helps teachers understand the developmental progression of QAR across the grade levels. For example, if first-grade teachers decide they want their students to know the two basic categories, In the Book and In My Head, their grade-level benchmark might read:

> Students will be able to generate and answer In the Book and In My Head questions based on first-grade texts.

If sixth-grade teachers notice that many of their students have trouble with Think & Search questions that occur frequently during content area assignments as well as on the state reading test, a grade-level benchmark might read:

> Students will be able to generate and answer Think & Search questions when reading sixth-grade fiction and nonfiction texts in all content areas.

Grade-level benchmarks may refer specifically to QAR, or they may refer to reading comprehension outcomes more generally. An example of the latter is seen in the following grade-level benchmark developed by first-grade teachers at a school in Hawaii:

> Students will be able to make inferences when reading a text.

These teachers found that giving students lessons about Author & Me helped their students to make inferences because making inferences requires students to blend information in the text with their own background knowledge (see Chapter 3). Though QAR isn't mentioned in the benchmark, it is the basis for instruction that helped students meet the benchmark.

It is important to consider the number of grade-level benchmarks related to reading comprehension. We've found that it is wise for teachers to begin by working with just one or two comprehension benchmarks. We make this recommendation for two reasons. First, as we noted in Chapter 3, comprehension strategies overlap and are highly interrelated. Teaching to a benchmark focusing on any particular comprehension strategy, such as distinguishing between main ideas and supporting details, almost always leads teachers to address other comprehension strategies, such as making inferences or monitoring comprehension. Second, in our experience with whole-school use of QAR, we have found that taking on a larger number of benchmarks that focus on single skills or strategies can overwhelm teachers and scatter their attention.

Student-Friendly "I Can" Statements

Teachers can then translate the professional language of benchmarks into student-friendly I Can statements. For example, kindergarten teachers translated the grade-level benchmark "Children will make and justify predictions about a text" into the following I Can statement:

> I can tell what will happen next in a story and why.

This I Can statement made the benchmark immediately understandable to students, although teachers also introduced students to the terms *justify* and *predictions*. Not surprisingly, rewording benchmarks into I Can statements is generally more important in the primary grades than in the upper elementary grades and above, where only slight changes to the wording may be needed. Also, some teachers prefer not to work out I Can statements in advance. Instead, they discuss the ideas behind the benchmark with students and ask them to help phrase the statements. With this approach students gain ownership over the I Can statements and are more likely to understand them. Once students know the expectations for their achievement, they are better able to take responsibility for their own learning. Moreover, we have found that I Can statements make the literacy-curriculum goals easily accessible to family members and others from the community who are involved in the students' education.

Karen Marfise, the third-grade teacher at Shields School introduced in Chapter 4, liked working with I Can statements because they provided her students with guidance and helped parents know the expectations. Hannah Natividad, Karen's colleague at Shields, found that her sixth-grade students referred to I Can statements and internalized them. She extended their use to science lessons, with statements such as "I know how a simple machine works." (Note that it is not always necessary to use the words *I can*.) Hannah saw that when parents asked, "What did you learn today?" her students could respond by talking about the I Can statement (these observations come from interviews conducted in late spring of the teachers' first year of using QAR schoolwide).

Sharing Benchmarks

Once benchmarks and I Can statements have been drafted for all grade levels, they can be shared with the whole school. The person facilitating the discussion helps teachers assess their grade-level benchmarks to see if they create the stepwise progression of achievement that characterizes the staircase curriculum. The teachers look at each benchmark to see if it will lead to improved reading comprehension and prepare students for the following year. Problems of repetition, omission, and discontinuity are commonly uncovered during the first round, and it is quite common to hold several rounds of discussion and revision before a staircase curriculum emerges. Teachers need to decide on the QAR categories to be introduced or emphasized at each grade level, along with related reading comprehension strategies and the types of texts students are expected to comprehend. QAR follows a developmental framework that points to specific categories and strategies relevant at various grade levels, but teachers need to use their professional judgment to formulate benchmarks appropriate for their students. For example, earlier we described some first-grade teachers who provided their students with instruction in Author & Me to enable them to make inferences, even though the category of Author & Me is not usually introduced until second or third grade, because they felt teaching about Author & Me was appropriate for their students at that time.

3. Monitoring Student Progress

Knowing what they are trying to accomplish leads teachers naturally to the next of the five phases: developing a system for monitoring students' progress toward these end-of-year goals. For example, fifth-grade teachers identified the following benchmark as central to their work for the year:

> Students will be able to generate and respond to Think & Search questions for nonfiction texts written for fifth graders.

They know their students often have difficulty applying what they have learned during reading instruction to content area learning. Within grade-level meetings, they explore their options: What are they already using that might serve as evidence of progress? What additional evidence might they want to collect? They consider the science and social studies textbooks that contain end-of-chapter questions and discuss whether they could ask students to identify the QAR for each question and then answer it. They consider adding a QAR component to the students' research reports. The students would be expected to generate questions and identify the QARs, then exchange reports so that they use each other's reports to answer the questions. Note that these teachers do not have to develop or purchase tests on QAR and reading comprehension. Instead they make use of students' ongoing work in the classroom. Evidence for this benchmark might come from sources such as end-of-chapter questions, inquiry questions, or literature response journals in which students have drafted questions to be discussed by their book clubs or student-led discussions. Often students are not even aware they are being assessed, because the teacher is simply collecting work that they would be doing as part of ongoing classroom instruction.

Teachers often find assessment to be a challenging topic. At Shields School, Jean Nielsen recalled that at first teachers felt overwhelmed by the idea of having to assess their students' progress on the grade-level benchmarks. Jean addressed the teachers' worries by reminding them that they didn't have to develop brand-new assessment procedures and that they should look at the assignments and work they already had in place.

Collecting Evidence

Identifying the evidence to use for monitoring is only part of the discussion. It is also important that all the teachers at a grade level agree on the procedures to be followed to collect the evidence, since they will be discussing and analyzing their results to determine their students' overall progress. If they do not follow the same procedures, they will not be able to compare and aggregate their results. For example, if teachers decide to use questions students have written for their research reports as evidence, they need to agree on the amount of time students have to generate those questions. The results will not be comparable across the grade if one teacher allows students only 30 minutes while another allows an hour. Teachers need to agree on the range of topics for the research reports because it may be easier for students to generate questions on some topics than on others. The degree of assistance available to students is also a factor—for example, whether students must generate the questions and QARs on their own or whether they are allowed to discuss their ideas with the teacher or a peer. Teachers at a given grade level often find it helpful to prepare a bulleted list of the procedures they will all follow to produce and collect benchmark evidence (see Figure 6.2).

Figure 6.2 *Example of Procedures for Collecting Evidence*

Procedures for Collecting Evidence

- *Assessment task*
  Students will state their prior knowledge about the topic. After finishing the entire story, students will restate the information that they read from the text.

Directions for Session 1

1. Explain the task.
2. Share the rubric.
3. Distribute the worksheet. Explain the writing task.
4. Have students write their personal knowledge about the topic.
5. Distribute the text.
6. Students complete their reading and restate in writing the information they read independently. Students are allowed to highlight and mark the text. Unlimited time.
7. Collect all materials.

Directions for Session 2

1. Explain the task and review the rubric.
2. Distribute materials.
3. Students write about how their personal knowledge about the topic was supported or changed because of new information learned from the text. Students summarize new information learned. Students review their worksheets and evaluate their work using the rubric and self-evaluation form.
4. Collect materials.

Created by Marelyn Manliguis, Kim Nakamura, Manford Realin, Laura Sakai, Grade 5 Teachers, Kipapa Elementary School, Mililani, Hawaii

Teachers also need to decide—as a whole school—how often they will collect evidence and share their students' results and the instructional decisions they have made based on their students' progress. For a schoolwide QAR program, we find it works well if teachers monitor student's progress three times per year through a pretest, midyear check, and posttest. Most schools establish a two-week window at each of these times for assessing students' progress. Teachers at most schools are already familiar with the idea of having a pretest and a posttest involving students in the same assessment tasks. We found it useful to add a midyear check of these same tasks. This allows teachers to make any necessary adjustments to instruction before the high-stakes testing that occurs in the spring in many districts.

Scoring With Rubrics

Next, teachers need to discuss how they will score the evidence they have collected. We recommend using a rubric or checklist that makes explicit what it would take to achieve end-of-year targets. Let's return to the fifth graders who need to be able to successfully generate and respond to Think & Search QARs in nonfiction contexts. The fifth-grade teachers may develop a rubric that would define success as follows: (1) the questions must require answer information found in their texts/reports, (2) a correct answer must involve synthesizing or summarizing text information, (3) the wording of the question must be easily understood and unambiguous, and so forth. The rubric may have three or four points for each feature, or the teachers may create a simple checklist of features that are present or absent.

Experienced teachers may be able to develop their scoring tool prior to administering the assessment for the first time. Other teachers may wish to collect the evidence and develop the rubric when they can refer to students' actual work. In either case, we recommend beginning with scoring tools that will determine whether students are

* working below the benchmark,
* meeting the benchmark, or
* exceeding the benchmark, defined as performing a year or more beyond the current grade level.

In our experience, it is not difficult for teachers to achieve agreement or reliability at a level of 90 percent or higher when scoring student work with rubrics of three levels. More levels can be added later, if necessary, although reliability becomes more difficult to achieve. A sample rubric is shown in Figure 6.3.

This rubric requires that teachers look at just a few features of students' work, including the quality of the questions and their QAR categories. Notice that, to be rated as having met the benchmark, students must show that they can comprehend a nonfiction text written at their grade level.

Figure 6.3 *A Typical Fifth-Grade Rubric*

Benchmark: Students will be able to answer and generate Think & Search questions based on the important information in nonfiction text written for fifth graders.

Working On	Meeting	Exceeding
• Unable to provide a complete and correct answer to Think & Search questions. May provide a partial answer or a mix of accurate and inaccurate information. Shows poor reasoning. • Unable to generate Think & Search questions. May provide another kind of question or a question that does not address information in the text. • Able to answer and generate Think & Search questions but only when based on text written below the fifth-grade level.	• Able to answer Think & Search questions based on nonfiction text written at the fifth-grade level. Answers are accurate but may include some unnecessary details. Answers convey the proper information but may not be well organized. • Able to generate Think & Search questions based on nonfiction text written at the fifth-grade level. Questions are based on important information and not minor details.	• Able to answer Think & Search questions based on nonfiction text written above the fifth-grade level. Answers include a well-structured synthesis or summary that addresses important points and leaves out extraneous information. • Able to generate Think & Search questions based on nonfiction text written above the fifth-grade level. Questions are based on main or important ideas rather than details.

Sometimes teachers ask how a student's work should be rated if it shows a good working knowledge of QAR when applied to a text written at a lower reading level (for example, a fifth grader who has read a text typically used in the third grade). The answer depends on what teachers expect of students with that particular benchmark. In some cases teachers want to focus on students' understanding of QAR and not on decoding ability. Other teachers believe that students must be able to apply QAR to texts written at their own grade level. While we can see good arguments on both sides of this issue, we tend to side with the second position and to believe that, with the exception of entering first graders, the benchmarks should be geared to have students independently read and comprehend texts at their grade level.

Grade-Level Sharing

After teachers have scored their students' work, they prepare bar graphs of the results. These allow teachers to see the overall progress

Figure 6.4 *A Sample Bar Graph*

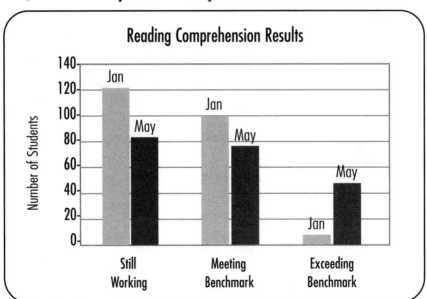

of the class in terms of the number of students in the categories of working on, meeting, and exceeding the grade-level benchmark. A sample bar graph showing reading comprehension results is presented in Figure 6.4.

Since this was Shields School's first year in the process, the teachers did not begin collecting evidence until January, after they had spent time developing their vision, benchmarks, and I Can statements. This graph illustrates how student performance improved. Notice how the number of students who were working on the comprehension benchmark decreased between January and May, with related increases in the numbers who met or exceeded the standard.

Bar graphs such as these formed the basis for the whole-school sharing that occurred in January and May. Teachers at Shields did have an early fall, whole-school sharing as well, but that one focused on developing the curriculum, not assessment. At Shields School, teachers found it beneficial to hear about the results from all the grade levels. For example, the eighth-grade teachers could learn about what the first-grade teachers were doing in terms of QAR. Everyone appreciated this opportunity, second-grade teacher Karen Mangin said, because each grade level could become aware of what all the other grade levels expected of the students.

Jennifer McClorey, the first-grade teacher at Shields who developed the QAR flip cards, commented that she and her colleagues experienced success by using a combination of I Can statements and rubrics worded in language students would understand. Previously, rubrics had been used by teachers but not students. Jennifer and her colleagues found that by rewriting rubrics so they were student friendly, students were able to engage in self-assessment, evaluating their strengths and weaknesses according to the rubric and setting goals for their own learning.

Teachers use student work collected as assessment evidence to identify the needs of the whole class, subgroups, and individuals and then improve instruction—the fifth phase of the schoolwide process. They prepare an analysis of students' strengths and weaknesses and decide on the kinds of instruction needed to move students forward with QAR and reading comprehension. For example, a group of third-grade teachers found that the majority of their students could formulate answers to Think & Search and Author & Me questions but were not taking the additional step of justifying their answers with information from the text. These teachers decided that they would teach students to do so by conducting lessons on quoting from the text, paraphrasing the text, and providing the numbers of the pages where the information was located.

4. Reporting Results to the Whole School

Schools successful in using QAR to improve schoolwide literacy instruction set aside time to share their pretest results, their midyear check results, and end-of-year posttest results. This sharing, the fourth phase in the process, requires that teachers prepare their data. These presentations may take various forms. Teachers at many schools have found it easiest to use PowerPoint or similar software that allows revisions and updates to be made easily. Some teachers prefer to use overhead transparencies, notebooks, or tri-fold boards to display their results. The photos in Figure 6.5 illustrate two formats. The first shows a series of tri-fold displays, each representing a different grade level. The second one shows the beginning of a teacher's bar graphs, in which she has recorded each child's score on an initial assessment. As the year progressed and more assessments were given, the teacher created bar graphs to show students' movement between the three rubric levels.

These presentations should contain the key information that other teachers will need to interpret the results. This information usually includes the state standard for reading comprehension, the grade-level benchmarks that correspond to the state standards, the student-friendly I Can statements, the evidence, the procedures for collecting evidence, the rubrics or other scoring tools, the bar graphs, instructional improvements, and any reflections.

Figure 6.5 *Examples of Grade-Level Displays for Whole-School Reporting*

Impact of QAR on Teachers and Students

In an interview that took place at the end of their first year of using QAR on a schoolwide basis at Shields School, Jean Nielsen described the effects on teachers and in classrooms. She noted that first and foremost, she saw evidence that teachers within and across grade levels had bought into the program. As she visited the classrooms, she noticed that all teachers had put up posters of QAR appropriate for their grade levels. She observed teachers conducting QAR lessons. She heard QAR being mentioned when teachers talked among themselves over lunch, and their comments, she thought, showed their understanding of and ownership of the initiative. The Shields teachers were able to begin developing a staircase curriculum for reading comprehension, so that every grade level had its own benchmarks and these benchmarks all contributed to the vision of the excellent reader.

More Focused Teaching

Fourth-grade teacher Victor Arroyo noted that after QAR was introduced the teachers at his grade level became more focused about what they were going to teach in reading comprehension and how they were going to teach it. As Jean noted, teachers were using QAR to frame comprehension instruction in ways that supported students' learning from text. Many teachers, during interviews at the end of their first year, described specific examples of individual students' learning, as well as general observations they had made of their classrooms.

For example, with the goals clearly laid out for his grade level, Victor was able to move his students away from trying to simply get the answer right to providing justifications for why they had chosen a particular answer. His students came to understand that their peers' answers might be different from their own as a result of their different knowledge and experience. Victor described a typical classroom scene now that his students understood QAR: A student generated a question, provided an answer, and explained how she had figured it out. She described the QAR as Think & Search, and she then talked about the strategies she had used to look for information in different parts of the text. Victor liked the fact that QAR helped his students understand both fiction and nonfiction and think about the process of comprehension, not simply find answers.

Help for Struggling Learners

Jennifer McClorey described how QAR instruction helped a struggling learner in her first-grade classroom. This boy had some speech difficulties and was very nervous about answering questions in class. A few weeks after Jennifer introduced the categories of In My Head and In the Book, she noticed that he was no longer intimidated by questions. He could figure out the QAR and then answer the question. She believed that QAR played an important part in starting this boy on the path to becoming a successful student.

Karen Mangin observed that her students had tended to ask low-level, Right There questions during guided reading and book discussions before she introduced them to QAR. She used the QAR vocabulary to guide them to develop thoughtful questions, and she saw their comprehension improve in all subject areas. As in Jennifer's classroom, a struggling learner in Karen's classroom became more comfortable participating in classroom discussions after he learned QAR. In fact, he helped other students with the technique.

Decreased Test Anxiety

Karen Marfise, the third-grade teacher who taught her students about writing from historical artifacts (as described in Chapter 4), found, following instruction, that her students used the language of QAR on their own and that they knew exactly what they were talking about. For example, during student-led discussions she noticed students telling each other, "That's not a Right There; that's an Author & Me." Her students felt empowered when taking tests because they could identify the QAR. If they came across a Right There question, they knew they could check the text for the answer. When Karen was preparing her students for the state test, one of the boys asked, "Are all of the questions going to be Right There?" Karen replied no, that there would be Author & Me and Think & Search questions too. Milagros Vazzano, the third-grade bilingual teacher at Shields, agreed that QAR had helped students with the state test. She noted that though some of the texts were two or three pages long, her students were not intimidated.

Cross-Grade and Cross-Curricular Applications

In a whole-school approach to implementing QAR, students benefit because they learn the language of QAR at one grade level and have that language, as well as their strategies for reading comprehension, extended in the following grade levels. For example, first graders who already know the broad category of In the Book will be able to learn the categories of Right There and Think & Search quickly in second grade. Milagros Vazzano understood that the instruction she provided in third grade would be different in the program's second year, when students would arrive in her classroom already familiar with QAR. It would be easy for her to build on the foundation already in place, and she might be able to move students farther along in reading comprehension. Milagros noted that she found it easy to teach QAR in Spanish, because the concepts remained the same and could readily be translated (see Figure 6.6).

Hannah Natividad recalled that many of her students began the year with the misconception that they were reading only to find

Figure 6.6 *QAR Chart With Spanish Translations*

answers. Hannah wanted her students to learn that reading is less about finding answers than about making connections from text to self, text to text, and text to world. Hannah felt that QAR helped her students develop into better readers by making them slow down and reflect on the reading process. In student-led discussions, students who had the job of discussion director knew they should create On My Own or Author & Me questions.

Teachers noted that students had internalized the language they had been taught related to QAR. For example, during a science lesson Hannah asked her students, "How did the universe come to be?" One of the students asked if this was an On My Own question because it seemed the teacher wanted to know the students' opinions. Hannah was able to use QAR language to clarify that she was actually asking an Author & Me. She wanted them to form an opinion based on what they had been studying. Jean recalled a Shields student who said about QAR, "Well, you know, once I get it, I can use it for other stuff." This student anticipated having the ability to apply QAR across the curriculum. Milagros described a case in which a student applied her knowledge of QAR outside of the classroom. The girl and her mother had gone to a restaurant, and the mother asked her the price of an item. The girl replied, "It's Right There," and her mother said, "What are you talking about?" The girl told Milagros, "She didn't know what I was talking about, but I did."

Concluding Comments

In this chapter we described how QAR could be adopted on a schoolwide basis to improve students' literacy achievement, particularly in the important area of reading comprehension. We described the importance of strong leadership to a school's progress, especially the role of the curriculum leader in coordinating efforts to develop a curriculum that builds from one grade to the next. We emphasized the critical importance of involving all teachers in the effort from the very start. Schools can find success with QAR by following a five-phase process that involves teachers in (1) understanding the big picture of reading, (2) setting goals for student learning, (3) monitoring student progress, (4) reporting results to the whole school, and (5) improving instruction. Using examples from actual schools, we described the positive impact that whole-school change centered on QAR has had on teachers and students, including many students of diverse cultural and linguistic backgrounds.

Chapter 7

Teacher Study Group Guide

*I*n this guide we present options for teachers in study groups who want to read and learn more about Question Answer Relationships. For each chapter, we provide two categories of guidance. First are guiding questions for use before, during, and after reading each chapter. The before-reading questions are designed to be used both at the end of each study group session to prompt group discussion of the upcoming chapter, and at the start of each chapter by individual readers working on their own. The during-reading questions are designed to promote deeper thinking about the content of the chapter. We recommend maintaining a reading log for recording responses to questions and new questions. The after-reading questions are designed to prompt initial discussion during the study group's meeting, as well as to supplement the questions generated by study group members. Many of these are a composite of questions we have been asked over the years as we worked with teachers learning about QAR or working to adapt it to particular teaching and learning situations. Second, we include a list of suggested activities intended to help our readers acquire personal experiences with questioning and QAR—with the ultimate goal of improving their instructional practices and engaging in deeper analysis of students' learning.

Chapter 1: Understanding Question Answer Relationships

Questions

Before reading:

1. What do you know about Question Answer Relationships? What do you hope to accomplish by participating in this study group and reading *QAR Now*?

2. Discuss with your study group your prior knowledge about QAR, including any experience you have from your college courses, your own professional reading, or your classroom experience.

During reading:

1. Keep track of questions that come up in your own mind as you read.

2. If you have already heard about QAR, list at least one thing that you read about in the chapter that surprised you.

After reading:

1. How has your teaching been affected by state and/or federal mandates that have increased the test-taking requirements for your students?

2. What tools do you feel you have that help you meet the challenges that stem from new federal and state mandates?

3. Think about the diversity of students in your classroom (or school). In what ways do you see the achievement gap playing out for your students? What kinds of systems does your school have in place to ensure that all students—from the highest achievers to the struggling learners—enjoy success and achieve end-of-year goals for learning?

4. In which instructional settings in your classroom do you think QAR will be most helpful? Generally helpful? A little helpful? Useful if adapted in a particular way?

Activities

1. Use the following sample text to practice developing material for introducing students to QAR. Focus on exploring with your colleagues how to create questions with answers that correspond relatively unambiguously to specific QARs. As a first step, create a three-column chart to use in working with the "Surfing the Sky" text below (from Raphael & Au, 2001).

Surfing the Sky

With a snowboard fastened to your feet, you hop to the open door of the airplane. The wind whips your face and pulls at your body. The ground far below looks like a bright green carpet. You jump and start surfing the air.

After jumping out of the plane, you are in freefall. Going through the air without a parachute for about 70 seconds, your body moves at 125 miles per hour.

Sky surfing is performed by a team of two athletes, a sky surfer and a camera flier. The team dives out of a plane flying 13,000 feet above the ground.

Label the first column "Question and Answer," the second "QAR," and the third "Comprehension Strategy." Create one question for each of the four core QARs. Then write the question and answer in the first column. Complete the chart by listing the QAR you believe each question represents and the comprehension strategy you used to answer it. Share your questions with your peers and ask them to do the same: Answer the question, identify the QAR, and note the comprehension strategy they used. Compare your answers and QARs and discuss similarities and differences in your interpretations.

2. Find an appropriate grade-level text that you plan to use in your classroom in the next week or so. Look through the text for a section to "lift." It should be a section for which you can create questions to contrast (*a*) In the Book and In My Head, (*b*) Right There and Think & Search, or (*c*) Author & Me and On My Own. Use a chart such as the one described in the first activity to record your questions, answers, QARs, and, if you choose, strategies for answering the question. (Note: This activity is also appropriate for Chapter 3, with its focus on comprehension.) Using the lifted text, write one question of each QAR type. Challenge your students to do the same, using either the lifted text or the rest of the text from which you lifted your section. Ask them to work in pairs to answer each other's questions, identify the QAR, and justify their choice of QAR. As your students work, roam the room so you can pick up on any misunderstandings they have.

3. Keep track of the variety of questions you encounter in one day. Discuss the information sources for answering those questions. Did all your questions fit into one of the four categories? If not, talk about why they didn't fit and which category they best approximate.

Chapter 2:
How to Teach QAR Lessons: A Six-Step Model

Questions

Before reading:

1. What are two important beliefs you have about teaching? About learning? About literacy and its goals?

2. Which instructional tools do you rely on as you design your curriculum and your daily lessons?

During reading:

1. Keep track of questions that come up in your own mind as you read.

2. Think about the beliefs you listed before reading. As you read, think about the theoretical background of QAR presented in the chapter. Which points do you find you connect with easily? With which points do you disagree?

3. Think about a successful literacy lesson you've taught. Which features of that lesson reflect elements of the six-step model?

After reading:

1. Think about the Vygotsky Space and the quadrants it describes. How do these four spaces play out in your classroom during literacy teaching and learning? During other school subjects?

2. Think about the processes of internalization, transformation, publication, and conventionalization. How have you seen these play out in your classroom?

3. Consider instances when you have used a gradual-release-of-responsibility approach during instruction. If you haven't used this model, what are some opportunities you have in your classroom to follow the six-step approach?

4. What participation structures are already in place in your classroom? Which ones do you feel foster higher levels of thinking in your students? How can you extend these kinds of interactions to other parts of the day?

5. How is teaching QAR helping you use a variety of participation structures in your teaching? In what ways are you extending what you are learning to other instructional contexts?

6. Are all of your students actively involved in your QAR lessons? If not, what changes can you make to involve them? Do you think cultural or linguistic differences are affecting their involvement?

Activities

1. In the coming week or month, look for situations in which you and your student(s) move through the gradual release of responsibility. Make notes of these examples to share and discuss at the next study group.

2. Look for examples of students' moving through the Vygotsky Space in your classroom this week or month. Make notes of these examples to share and discuss with the study group.

3. Focus on a struggling reader (or an English language learner, special education student, beginning reader, etc.) as you teach higher-level thinking concepts in QAR. What do you notice about his or her ability to engage with, understand, and learn complex concepts?

4. Design a QAR lesson with all six steps outlined in the chapter, using Figure 2.5 as a guide. With a teaching partner, talk through the lesson before you teach it, making sure that all six steps are included. Teach the lesson (or series of lessons) while your teaching partner observes. After the lesson, sit with your partner and discuss your teaching, the six steps, and what you learned about your own teaching during the process. Ask your teaching partner to listen in a nonjudgmental way while you analyze both the strong and weak points of the lesson. Next, ask your partner to give you feedback on the lesson's strengths and weaknesses. If you and your partner teach at the same grade level, you may want to plan a six-step QAR lesson together, then watch each other teach it. The second person to teach the lesson should benefit from the first person's experience.

5. Audiotape or videotape yourself during a Think Aloud lesson. As you listen or watch the tape, what do you notice? Do you switch to lower-level telling at any point? You might want to consider doing this kind of analysis of classroom talk—yours and your students' talk—in other contexts as well, such as guided reading, shared reading, or a content area lesson.

Chapter 3:
How QAR Frames Comprehension Instruction

Questions

Before reading:

1. Do you recall any class in which you were taught comprehension strategies? If so, discuss that experience. If you were never taught comprehension strategies, discuss possible reasons for the absence of this type of instruction.

2. Which comprehension strategies do you teach? How do you teach them? How do you assess whether or not students are making appropriate strategy choices in their own reading?

3. Which comprehension strategies do you think align with before, during, and after reading?

During reading:

1. Keep track of questions and comments you have on various sections of the text.

2. What other experiences have you had—reading, professional development sessions, etc.—that relate to the ideas in this chapter?

3. Maintain a list of strategies you have used to make connections to what you already know about comprehension and between ideas within the text. In particular, focus on how each strategy helps you manage information from the book and from your background knowledge.

After reading:

1. In what ways are you beginning to see the language of QAR become a part of the culture of your classroom? As you notice examples of this happening, write them down so you can share with the group.

2. How does thinking about comprehension strategies in the context of the reading cycle change how you might teach them?

Activities

1. Find a text that is at your own level (an adult book, a professional book, a journal article, etc.). Take notes about the questions you find yourself asking before, during, and after you read it. In what ways are your questions similar to those of your students? In what ways are they different?

2. Choose a content area in which you would like to embed some QAR instruction in a consistent and systematic manner. Plan how you will thread QAR language and talk throughout the lesson and in the questions that are asked as a part of that lesson. Teach the lesson and reflect on the integration of QAR into your teaching. What effect does this integration have on your classroom language and culture?

Chapter 4:
Teaching QAR Across Grades and Content Areas

Questions

Before reading:

1. How much QAR knowledge do your current students (or the students coming to you next year) have? Are they likely to be new to QAR instruction? Do they have a firm grasp of QAR? How will this affect your instruction?

2. How do you think QAR instruction should differ from first to third to fifth grade? Could students in high school benefit from QAR instruction? How? Why?

3. How do you think QAR instruction should change throughout the school year?

During reading:

1. Make text-to-self connections as you read about teachers and students at different grade levels and in different subject areas. How are you similar to or different from the examples? What implications do these differences or similarities have for how you would teach QAR?

2. What other experiences have you had—reading, professional development sessions, etc.—that relate to the ideas in this chapter?

After reading:

1. How does the amount of QAR background knowledge your students have impact your plan for introducing, teaching, and extending QAR in your classroom?

2. What examples from the chapter directly apply to your planning for a year of QAR instruction at your level (primary, intermediate, etc.)?

3. How else can you extend QAR into your classroom instruction (science, social studies, math, literacy)?

Activities

1. Develop a grade-level plan to implement QAR across the year. Meet with teachers from grade levels above and below yours as you are making your plan. It is important to have conversations about students' developing knowledge and appropriate transitions in learning. Think about the developmental needs of your students, their prior knowledge of QAR, and their grade level. What QAR categories should be taught at your grade level? How can QAR best be introduced at your grade level?

2. Think about a content area that you currently teach (science, social studies, math, art, etc.). How can you use QAR to make different content area connections (as Karen or Hannah did)?

Chapter 5: QAR and Test Preparation

Questions

Before reading:

1. How do you prepare your students for standardized and district-mandated tests? About how much instructional time do you spend on test preparation?

2. How effective do you think your current test-preparation lessons are? What areas would you like to improve?

3. Describe the degree of pressure you (as a classroom teacher, school literacy coordinator, administrator) feel to move students toward higher achievement on the high-stakes tests they must take? Describe the effects these tests have on the instructional decisions you make.

4. Which teachers in your school take responsibility for ensuring that students are learning the content for high-stakes tests? How do you fit into the bigger picture of test preparation in your school?

During reading:

1. Keep track of questions and comments you have on various sections of the text.

2. What other experiences have you had—reading, professional development sessions, etc.—that relate to the ideas in this chapter?

After reading:

1. Are you aware of the specific content standards that are tested at your grade level? How are these content standards integrated into

your instruction? Think about how these standards affect your instruction in the classroom and your plan for teaching QAR.

2. How are your state tests scored? Has any staff member been trained as a scorer or attended workshops on scoring practices? How can this information be helpful as you plan QAR instruction?

Activities

1. Give your students a text and questions about it to answer. Ask them one-on-one to tell you how they found the answers. Are your students naming comprehension strategies and thinking aloud? Can they name the sources of information they used to answer the questions?

2. Find recently released items from your state department of education's Web site for your grade level. Discuss the task demands these items place on your students.

3. Find the state content standards for each grade level at which the students in your school will be tested. Meet in grade-level teams to discuss how these standards are covered across a student's entire schooling experience.

4. Analyze released items and determine the types of QARs your students will encounter. Are there QAR types that seem to appear more often than others? Less often?

5. Remove any indication of the grade levels from passages in released state test items. Have your study group try to determine the level of the text. Discuss the results and the implications these levels have on classroom instruction and test preparation.

Chapter 6: The Benefit of Whole-School Adoption of QAR

Questions

Before reading:

1. What are teachers at each grade level in your school doing to teach reading comprehension? Is comprehension instruction coordinated across grade levels?

2. Do you see the need to improve reading comprehension instruction at your school? What steps do you think would help?

3. What whole-school changes, if any, has your school already attempted? What were the results of these efforts? If the changes were successful, what factors contributed to that success? If unsuccessful, what factors contributed to the poor results?

During reading:

1. Keep track of questions and comments you have on various sections of the text.

2. What other experiences have you had—reading, professional development sessions, etc.—that relate to the ideas in this chapter?

3. As you note the phases of school change and the associated components—such as the vision statement that describes the excellent reader who graduates from the school or the end-of-year targets and related assessment system—think about the components you believe you and your school have in place already and what you would need to develop.

After reading:

1. What new ideas did you learn about successful whole-school change efforts? How can you apply this knowledge in your school?

2. What would it take for QAR to be used as a framework for whole-school change in your setting? What could you do to support such an effort?

3. How do the results obtained in other schools with QAR instruction compare with the experiences of teachers and students in your school?

Activities

1. Map out a step-by-step plan for whole-school change based on QAR. List the assets for reform in place at your school. List the obstacles and think of ways these obstacles may be surmounted.

2. Plan a 30-minute workshop to introduce parents to QAR. If possible, test your workshop with a small group of parents and report the results to the study group.

Bibliography

Children's Books Cited

Ada, A. F. (1999). *My Name Is Mar'a Isabel*. New York: Aladdin.

dePaola, T. (1998). *Nana Upstairs and Nana Downstairs*. New York: G. P. Putnam's Sons.

MacLachlan, P. (1987). *Sarah Plain and Tall*. New York: HarperTrophy.

Moss, M. (2002). *Hannah's Journal*. Madison, WI: Turtleback Books.

Reynolds, P. N. (1991). *Shiloh*. New York: Atheneum.

Ryan, P. M. (2000). *Esperanza Rising*. New York: Scholastic, Inc.

Professional References

Allington, R. L. (1983). The reading instruction provided readers of different reading abilities. *Elementary School Journal, 83*, 549–559.

Anderson, R. C., & Pearson, P. D. (1984). A schema-theoretic view of basic processes in reading comprehension. In P. D. Pearson (Ed.), *Handbook of reading research* (pp. 255–292). New York: Longman.

Anderson, R.C., Spiro, R.J., & Montague, W.E. (Eds.). (1977). *Schooling and the acquisition of knowledge*. Mahwah, NJ: Erlbaum.

Au, K. H. (1993). *Literacy instruction in multicultural settings*. Fort Worth, TX: Harcourt Brace Jovanovich College Publishers.

Au, K. H. (2003). Literacy research and students of diverse backgrounds: What does it take to improve achievement? In C. M. Fairbanks, J. Worthy, B. Maloch, & J. Hoffman (Eds.), *52nd yearbook of the National Reading Conference* (pp. 85–91). Oak Creek, WI: National Reading Conference.

Au, K. H. (2006). *Multicultural issues and literacy achievement*. Mahwah, NJ: Erlbaum.

Au, K. H. (2006). Negotiating the slippery slope: School change and literacy achievement. *Journal of Literacy Research, 37*(3), 267–288.

Au, K. H., Hirata, S., & Raphael, T. E. (2005). Improving literacy achievement through standards. *California Reader, 39*(1), 5–10.

Au, K. H., & Mason, J. M. (1981). Social organizational factors in learning to read: The balance of rights hypothesis. *Reading Research Quarterly, 17*(1), 115–152.

Au, K. H., & Raphael, T. E. (1998). Curriculum and teaching in literature-based programs. In T. E. Raphael & K. H. Au (Eds.), *Literature-based instruction: Reshaping the curriculum* (pp. 123–148). Norwood, MA: Christopher-Gordon.

Benito, Y. M., Foley, C. L., Lewis, C. D., & Prescott, P. (1993). The effect of instruction in question answer relationships and metacognition on social studies comprehension. *Journal of Research in Reading,* 16(1), 20–29.

Brown, A. L., Armbruster, B. B., & Baker, L. (1986). The role of metacognition in reading and studying. In J. Orasanu (Ed.), *Reading comprehension: From research to practice* (pp. 49–75). Hillsdale, NJ: Erlbaum.

Brown, A. L., Campione, J. C., & Day, J. D. (1981). Learning to learn: On training students to learn from texts. *Educational Researcher,* 10, 14–21.

Darling-Hammond, L. (1995). Inequality and access to knowledge. In J. A. Banks & C. A. M. Banks (Eds.), *Handbook of research on multicultural education* (pp. 465–483). New York: Macmillan.

Dole, J. A., Duffy, G. G., Roehler, L. R., & Pearson, P. D. (1991). Moving from the old to the new: Research on reading comprehension instruction. *Review of Educational Research,* 61(2), 239–264.

Duke, N. K., & Pearson, P. K. (2002). Effective practices for developing reading comprehension. In A. E. Farstrup & S. J. Samuels (Eds.), *What research has to say about reading instruction* (pp. 205–242). Newark, DE: International Reading Association.

Durkin, D. (1978–1979). What classroom observations reveal about reading comprehension instruction. *Reading Research Quarterly,* 15, 481–533.

Ezell, H. K., Hunsicker, S. A., Quinque, M. M., & Randolph, E. (1996). Maintenance and generalization of QAR reading comprehension strategies. *Reading Research and Instruction,* 36(1), 64–81.

Ezell, H. K., Hunsicker, S. A., & Quinque, M. M. (1997). Comparison of two strategies for teaching reading comprehension skills. *Education and Treatment of Children,* 20(4), 365–382.

Ezell, H. K., Kohler, F. W., Jarzynka, M., & Strain, P. S. (1992). Use of peer-assisted procedures to teach QAR reading comprehension strategies to third-grade children. *Education and Treatment of Children, 15*(3), 205–227.

Fitzgerald, J. (1995). English-as-a-second-language reading instruction in the United States: A research review. *Journal of Reading Behavior, 27,* 115–152.

Florida comprehensive assessment test, grade 8 reading released items (2001, Spring). Retrieved July 4, 2005, from the Florida Information Resource network Web site: http://www.firn.edu/doe/sas/fcat/pdf/fc8rib1r.pdf.

Gavelek, J. R., & Raphael, T. E. (1996). Changing talk about text: New roles for teachers and students. *Language Arts, 73*(3), 182–192.

Graham, L., & Wong, B. Y. L. (1993). Comparing two modes of teaching a question-answering strategy for enhancing reading comprehension: Didactic and self-instructional training. *Journal of Learning Disabilities, 26*(4), 270–279.

Grigg, W. S., Daane, M. C., Jin, Y., & Campbell, J. R. (2003). *The nation's report card: Reading 2002* (NCES 2003-521). Washington, DC: U.S. Department of Education, Institute of Education Sciences.

Griggens, S. (2001). Extreme sports. In T. E. Raphael & K. H. Au, *Super QAR for testwise students, grade 5.* Chicago: McGraw-Hill/Wright Group.

Guthrie, J. T., & Wigfield, A. (2000) Engagement and motivation in reading. In M. L. Kamil, B. P. Mosenthal, P. D. Pearson, & R. Barr (Eds.), *Handbook of reading research* (Vol. III, pp. 403–422) Mahwah, NJ: Erlbaum.

Hansen, J., & Pearson, P. D. (1983). An instructional study: Improving the inferential comprehension of good and poor fourth-grade readers. *Journal of Educational Psychology, 75,* 821–829.

Harré, R. (1984). *Personal being: A theory for individual psychology.* Cambridge, MA: Harvard University Press.

Harvey, S., & Goudvis, A. (2000). *Strategies that work.* York, ME: Stenhouse.

Highfield, K. (2003). Test preparation in two contexts. Unpublished dissertation, Oakland University, Rochester, MI.

Jensen, N. (2001). Qillak. In T. E. Raphael & K. H. Au., *Super QAR for testwise students.* Chicago, IL: McGraw-Hill/Wright Group.

Lipson, M. Y. (1983). The influence of religious affiliation on children's memory for text information. *Reading Research Quarterly, 18,* 448–457.

National Assessment Governing Board (2004). *Reading framework for the 2009 national assessment of educational progress* (Contract No. ED-02-R-0007). Washington, DC: American Institutes for Research.

National Center for Educational Statistics (2003). *2003 reading assessment.* Washington, DC: U.S. Department of Education, Institute of Education Sciences.

Newmann, F. M., Smith, B. S., Allenworth, E., & Bryk, A. S. (2001). Instructional program coherence: What it is and why it should guide school improvement policy. *Educational Evaluation and Policy Analysis*, 23(4), 297–321.

Oakes, J., & Guiton, G. (1995). Matchmaking: The dynamics of high school tracking decisions. *American Educational Research Journal*, 32(1), 3–33.

Ogle, D. M. (1986). K-W-L: A teaching model that develops active reading of expository text. *The Reading Teacher*, 39(6), 564–570.

Paris, S. G., Lipson, M. Y., & Wixson, K. K. (1983). Becoming a strategic reader. *Contemporary Educational Psychology*, 8, 293–316.

Pearson, P. D. (1985). Changing the face of reading comprehension instruction. *The Reading Teacher*, 38(6), 724-738.

Pearson, P. D., & Duke, N. K (2002). *Comprehension instruction: Best research-based practices.* New York: Guilford Press.

Pearson, P. D., & Fielding, L. (1991). Comprehension instruction. In R. Barr, M. L. Kamil, P. Mosenthal, & P. D. Pearson (Eds.), *Handbook of reading research* (Vol. II, pp. 819–860). New York: Longman.

Pearson, P. D., & Johnson, D. D. (1978). *Teaching reading comprehension.* New York: Holt, Rinehart and Winston.

Pressley, M. (2002). Comprehension strategies instruction. In C. C. Block & M. Pressley (Eds.), *Comprehension instruction: Research-based best practices* (pp. 11–27). New York: Guilford Press.

Raphael, T. E. (1986). Teaching question answer relationships, revisited. *The Reading Teacher*, 39, 516–152.

Raphael, T. E. & Au, K. H. (2001). *Super QAR for testwise students, Grades 1–8.* Chicago: McGraw-Hill/Wright Group.

Raphael, T. E., & Au, K. H. (2005). QAR: Enhancing comprehension and test-taking across grades and content areas. *The Reading Teacher*, 59(3) 206–221.

Raphael, T. E., & Brock, C. H. (1997). Instructional research in literacy: Changing paradigms. In C. Kinzer, D. Leu, & K. Hinchman (Eds.), *Inquiries in literacy theory and practice* (pp. 16–36). Chicago: National Reading Conference.

Raphael, T. E., Florio-Ruane, S., George, M., Hasty, N. L., & Highfield, K. (2004). *Book club plus: A literacy framework for the primary grades.* Lawrence, MA: Small Planet Communications.

Raphael, T. E., & McKinney, J. M. (1983). An examination of 5th and 8th grade children's question answering behavior: An instructional study in metacognition. *Journal of Reading Behavior* (now *Journal of Literacy Research*), 15, 67–86.

Raphael, T. E., & Pearson, P. D. (1985). Increasing students' awareness of sources of information for answering questions. *American Educational Research Journal,* 22(2), 217–235.

Raphael, T. E., & Wonnacott, C. A. (1985). Heightening fourth-grade students' sensitivity to sources of information for answering comprehension questions. *Reading Research Quarterly,* 20(3), 282–296.

Rodgers, E. (2004). Interactions that scaffold reading performance. *Journal of Literacy Research,* 36, 501–532.

Schank, R.C., & Abelson, R.P. (1977). *Scripts, plans, goals and understanding: an inquiry into human knowledge structures.* Mahwah, NJ: Erlbaum.

Schunk, D. H., & Zimmerman, B. J. (1997). Developing self-efficacious readers and writers: The role of social and self-regulatory processes. In J. T. Guthrie & A. Wigfield (Eds.), *Reading engagement: Motivating readers through integrated instruction* (pp. 14–33). Newark DE: International Reading Association.

Singer, H., & Donlan, D. (1982). Active comprehension: Problem-solving schema with question generation for comprehension of complex short stories. *Reading Research Quarterly,* 17, 166–186.

Stahl, N. (2002, February, 4). National Reading Conference. Message posted to NRCEMAIL electronic mailing list.

Sweet, A. P., & Snow, C. E. (Eds.). (2003). *Rethinking reading comprehension: Solving problems in teaching of literacy.* New York: Guilford Press.

Taylor, B. M., Pearson, P. D., Peterson, D. P., & Rodriguez, M. C. (2003). Reading growth in high-poverty classrooms: The influence of teacher practices that encourage cognitive engagement in literacy learning. *Elementary School Journal*, 104, 3–28.

Taylor, B. M., Pearson, P. D., Peterson, D. P., & Rodriguez, M. C. (2005). The CIERA school change framework: An evidence-based approach to professional development and school reading improvement. *Reading Research Quarterly*, 40(1), 40–69.

Taylor, B. M., Peterson, D. P., Pearson, P. D., & Rodriguez, M. C. (2002). Looking inside classrooms: Reflecting on the "how" as well as the "what" in effective reading instruction. *The Reading Teacher*, 56–79.

Vygotsky, L. S. (1981). The genesis of higher mental functions. In J. V. Wertsch (Ed.), *The concept of activity in psychology*. Armonk, NY: M. E. Sharpe.

Vygotsky, L. S. (1986). *Thought and language* (A. Kozulin, Trans.). Cambridge, MA: MIT Press.

Wood, B., Bruner, J. S., & Ross, G. (1976). The role of tutoring in problem solving. *Journal of Child Psychology and Psychiatry*, 17, 89–100.

Index

QAR Now: Question Answer Relationships